HOW TO SELECT WINNING STOCKS AND AVOID LOSERS

Copyright © 2018 Shmulik Karpf

All rights reserved.

ISBN: 1987592859

ISBN 13: 9781987592856

CreateSpace Independent Publishing Platform

DEDICATION

To my joyful daughter, Rona, who - like the stock market - never stops amazing me.

"The stock market is like an ocean – It is constantly changing, yet – it always remains the same".

CONTENTS

	Acknowledgments	I
1	The Ultimate Investing Principle	Pg 1
2	Step #1: Dominant position	Pg 5
3	Step #2: Free Cash Flow	Pg 16
4	Step #3: Shareholders in the center	Pg 24
5	Step #5: Valuation (How to make sure you're not overpaying for a business)	Pg 33
6	Step #6: The Catalyst behind the story	Pg 43
	Catalyst #1 - The "Revenue Disappointment" Catalyst	Pg 45
	Catalyst #2 - The "Event driven" Catalyst	Pg 74
	Catalyst #3 - The "Sector driven" Catalyst	Pg 107
7	Some final thought	Pg 120

INTRODUCTION

The stock market never stops surprising me - So many people coming to the same place with the same purpose – to make money. Yet, very few people succeed and make it to the finish line. Unfortunately, most investors end up losing money in the long run.

There are plenty of reasons why common investors rarely turn into winners in the ever-evolving stock market game. Some people do not have a "winning" formula. Others do have a formula that's working for them but for some reason, they don't seem to stick with it for the long haul. Some people, on the other hand, make enormous gains but then lose everything on a few silly bets. Other people don't know how to properly diversify their portfolio, and they expose themselves to tremendous risks.

I want to be very clear with you, right from the start. This book does not have a solution for greedy investors, for investors who believe that the stock market is a Russian roulette, and for investors who are constantly impatient and always look for action. This book, though, does have something very special to offer you, the person who wants to be highly successful in the stormy waters of the stock market.

In this book, I will describe and explain in detail my 5-step strategy for picking stocks. This strategy is the culmination of my years as an equity analyst at a major bank. I believe that this stock picking strategy is one of the safest investment strategies that you can possibly find. And even more importantly – It's relatively simple to implement.

Believe me; I have tried pretty much each and every investing strategy known to mankind. This strategy is the most lucrative strategy with the minimal risk out there. As simple as it may sound, my 5-step strategy is highly reliable. It has worked in both bear markets as well as bull markets. My strategy has beaten the major indices, year after year, and with lesser volatility than the volatility of the overall market.

But before we even get started, it's essential that I tell you what you should not expect from this book. This book isn't a quick "How to get rich in one year" guide, nor is it a "How to make 50% a year in the stock market" manual. If you're looking for such manual, kindly close this book and proceed down the aisle. I'm sure you'll find many such guides with tempting headlines there. The trouble with these books is that the most successful item in the book isn't the content but the headline. This type of "quick" guides usually leads to financial ruin to everyone but their highly motivated authors.

After we discussed what you should not expect from this

book, I can now tell you what you can and should expect from it. By reading my book, you will get access to my years of experience as an equity analyst. This experience, with its successes and failures, has been refined to 5 main investing rules. Giving you a 1,000-page guide to the stock market is easy. But giving you a detailed 5 rule strategy requires much more from me.

I will walk you through the nuts and bolts of my 5- step strategy for picking stocks. I will explain how this system works and how you can make it work for you. There's absolutely no reason why you shouldn't take advantage of my investing strategy and become a skilled stock picker. Now, if you've decided that you wish to give it a try, I'm more than glad to welcome you aboard. I urge you to pick up my book and begin to learn my steady, consistent way to stock market success.

CHAPTER 1:
THE ULTIMATE INVESTING PRINCIPLE

I don't personally believe in fast rules of thumb or in some magic formula that is the holy grail of investing. Those tricks never seem to work, or they sometimes appear to be working until they suddenly don't, and you end up losing money. These games are not for me.

Despite my dislike for fast rules, I do keep a special room in my heart for a principle that has always been the cornerstone of my analysis, and almost always spared me from losses. This principle might sound simplistic to you at first, but when you dive deep into its meaning, you'll find many truths that should be the cornerstone of every investing strategy.

The investing rule that I'm referring to is to always maintain a highly favorable risk-reward ratio.

It is common sense that if you want to win and keep winning, you must always make sure that the odds are stacked in your favor. The most straightforward way of stacking the odds in your favor is to make sure that the upside in your investment is at least twice the amount of downside that you might incur. I want to be very clear on this. This investing rule is not some cliché, it's very practical and down to earth.

Whenever I begin analyzing a company, I constantly ask myself what is the upside in this investment, or in other words, how undervalued I believe this stock really is. I do the math and I come up with a potential appreciation estimate. In most cases, I will not recommend a stock with less than 20 percent upside, at the least.

Now comes the more difficult, and arguably more important, part of this equation – the downside part. Once I conclude how much this security is worth, I must come up with an estimated value in case I'm wrong. You must always assume that the worst can happen. It isn't likely, you're hoping that it won't materialize, but things can definitely go south from here.

The tricky part is to try and provide a price estimate for what the shares would be worth if what you thought would happen, did not happen. In most cases, I will only recommend a stock with a potential downside of no greater than 10 percent.

To put it differently, I will not recommend a stock with a potential 40 percent upside and a 40 percent downside. That's a 1 to 1 ratio, and it isn't good enough for me. It is not really my cup of tea. In contrast, I would love to find opportunities with a 20 percent upside and a 10 percent downside, reflecting a 2 to 1 ratio. This way, you're the house and somebody else is the gambler.

Throughout this book, you'll get to explore many investment ideas which are very different from one another. The only common thread to all those investment ideas is that for each and any one of them, I applied the same investing rule – the favorable risk-reward profile. If the investment idea did not meet the required profile, it simply wasn't recommended, regardless of its upside potential.

More importantly, by applying my 5 investing rules – you will practically eliminate many different risks to your investment. The five rules are there to keep you out of harm's way.

Rule #1 is there to make sure you don't invest in small companies that might disappear overnight due to a weak balance sheet, lack of competitive advantage, or a combination of the two.

Rule #2 is there to make sure you aren't fooled by all sorts of tricky accounting. By sticking with companies that consistently exhibit a strong cash flow stream, you will always be certain that the profits are, in fact, real profits and not just seemingly real accounting profits.

Rule #3 is there to make sure the company doesn't turn its back on you. There are many profitable companies out there, but not all have your best interest at heart. By sticking with shareholder-friendly companies, you make sure that the company takes care of you, and not the other way around.

Rule #4 is there to make sure you don't hold a stock forever hoping that one day "it might go up". By setting a clearly defined catalyst, you know what to expect and you understand which events will trigger the "comeback" and are bound to propel the stock higher.

Rule #5 is there to make sure you always invest with a margin of safety. By making sure you pay a good price for a stock, rather than a hefty one, you are leaving some room for error, which is always a wise thing to do given the uncertainties of the stock market.

All in all, the purpose of the five steps is to make sure you buy the right stocks, at the right time, for the right price.

CHAPTER 2:
STEP #1: DOMINANT POSITION

As My first criterion, in choosing winning stocks and avoiding losers, is the dominance of the company in its field of business operations. To put differently, I must always determine whether the company I am about to invest in is a true leader in its field of business, or merely a potential "want to be". If you doubt this, somewhat rigid criteria, and perhaps believe that it is not so important, please take a minute to ponder about the fate of all those "would be" Googles in China or Russia. You could then take another minute and think what happened to all those beverage companies who tried to emulate Coca-Cola or Pepsi.

The straightforward answer to this question is that they are mostly extinct, embraced by insolvency, or simply went into oblivion at some point in time. Picking a leader, or one of the top leading companies in a given industry is an excellent recipe for avoiding all sorts of disasters.

Why is it so important to identify a dominant player?

The business environment is difficult enough. Corporate America has been consolidating for years now. The larger companies are buying out the smaller ones and becoming stronger and more influential. This isn't happening strictly in one sector but across various sectors of the market.

Dominant players have a strong edge. They usually have the financial ability to invest heavily in research and development (R&D), which creates an enormous future barrier for entry for other potential competitors. You see, not many companies can match Pfizer's 8$ billion annual investment in R&D. This staggering sum is much higher than the total market cap of many other smaller drug companies.

Another reason for picking leaders is not their line of operations, but their balance sheets. In most cases, the leading companies in a given industry will have less leveraged balance sheets and enjoy a stronger stream of cash flow. By focusing on the leaders, you will likely avoid the big troublemakers, those companies with too much debt, too little cash, and a strained balance sheet that might, in some cases, lead them to insolvency.

A third reason for picking leading companies is that the larger corporations usually attract a better-skilled workforce. Better resources and a long-standing reputation in the business attract the best employees, a thing which ensures better prospects for the business going forward. In addition, the sheer size of the corporation enables it to reach highly favorable terms with its contractors and suppliers.

All in all, a dominant corporation will hire better workers, incur fewer expenses and create a wide moat around its business in the form of a strong brand, substantial investments in R&D, or a high level of capital expenditures. So, a leading corporation is what you want to have in your portfolio, but how do you recognize one when you see it?

How to identify a leader in an industry

There are plenty of ways to recognize a leader. I will share five methods that I often use. You can use them in conjunction or as standalone criteria. I personally like to use all five of them.

The first method focuses on the companies that hold the greatest market share in their respective industry. The second method is less quantitative and more qualitative and aims at identifying the strongest brands in the industry. The third method attempts to distinguish businesses whose clients are "sticky" and are likely to return, from businesses whose clients are not "sticky". The fourth method analyzes the financials of leaders and distinguishes them from the financials of other non-leading businesses.

So, how do we identify a leader?

Method #1: percentage of Market share in the industry

The dominant player in the industry will usually be entitled to the lion's share of revenues. In today's world of easily accessible information on the internet, you really do not need to spend days over days of research in the library in order to find the leader. It's all at your reach while sipping coffee in your living room.

The easiest example of an undisputed leader can be found in the market for PC operating systems. Microsoft Corporation controls about ninety percent of the market. The rest is divided between Apple and other Linux based operating systems.

Now, we'll try and find the leader in a more complicated business environment. Let's say that you're a fan of alcoholic beverages in general, and of beer in particular. You really want to learn more about the global beer industry and the major players in the field. Let's also assume that you do not have the slightest idea as to what company manufactures your favorite beer, The Corona. A quick check on the internet informs you that Corona is not a standalone corporation. After a quick one minute search, you realize that the name of the company that manufactures The Corona is ABI Inbev, a massive beer conglomerate based in Brussels. So far, so good.

But how dominant is ABI Inbev within the global business of beer manufacturing? Well, it only sounds complicated. By clicking some very basic search words like "ABI + global market share" on Google, you quickly realize that the beer industry is highly concentrated. In fact, ABI used to control roughly 21 percent of the global beer market. Following the highly criticized buyout of SABMiller in 2016, its tough rival, the conglomerate now controls about 40 percent of the market. ABI is the undisputed global leader of the beer market.

Another example of a clear market leader is found in the communication equipment industry. How many companies do you think produce Ethernet switches and routing solutions? Well, quite a few actually. But this highly condensed market is controlled by the mighty Cisco who is responsible for 61 percent of total communication networking sales worldwide.

Checking the market share of companies in their respective industries provides you with a nice, clear insight into the business dynamics of the industry. Specifically, it will point towards the "gorillas in the room" of that industry. You can easily look up information on sites like Google, Statista, Markets, and IDC.

Method #2: Powerful brands

Do you like to eat chocolates? I know that I do. Specifically, I favor Lindt series of dark chocolates. If you did some basic homework on Lindt, you would find that it is a Swiss manufacturer of high-quality premium chocolates and that the company has been in business for over 120 years. Lindt is highly regarded for its brand of fine chocolates. In fact, Lindt has been able to steadily increase prices of its chocolates year in year out, regardless of the prices of cocoa. The only reason customers are willing to put up with Lindt's costly chocolates is that they regard them as superior quality relative to rival chocolate manufacturers.

Keep in mind that Lindt is a dominant player in its field of business, although its market share is far from being the highest in the category. Chocolate manufacturers such as Mars (private company), Mondelez (MDLZ) and Hershey's (HSY) comprise the biggest players in the chocolate category. Despite the fact that Lindt is not a leader in market share, it definitely enjoys a favorable status due to its very strong brand.

Louis Vuitton is another name that enjoys the status of a favorable brand. Its iconic bags, perfumes, and leather products are sold at imaginary prices. Just consider the fact that the company's most basic women's bag retails for

2,500$. In this case, it is the hefty price and the luxurious image that differentiates Louis Vuitton from other fashion brands.

Keep in mind, though, that easily recognizable brands are not always immune from danger. Shareholders of Hugo Boss or Michael Kors saw the company's share price plunge by over 50 percent over the past three years. Contrast that performance with that of shares of Louis Vuitton that appreciated by more than 50 percent during the same period. So, in choosing the market leader by brand power, you must pick easily recognizable, highly diversified, highly durable brands. Simply said, you have to pick the most recognizable brands, or the most luxurious, but not the most fashionable. Fashion changes often, but extra pricey fashion brands do tend to maintain their status.

Method #3: "Sticky clients"

This method of finding leading companies is highly qualitative. We try and find leaders by tracing their clients and then trying to determine whether these clients are one-of-a-time clients who are not likely to return, or whether we have got ourselves "sticky" clients who will come back to us to get more of the product we sell.

One classic field where we can find "sticky" clients is

the field of drugs and medicine. When a certain drug or a specific therapy proves to be effective, clients are not likely to go out searching for some other, creative medical solutions, even if the current drug or therapy is highly expensive.

Let's use an example. Back in August 2015, I initiated a "buy" recommendation on Baxter (BAX), a medical device company with a very specific niche. Its specialty was in assisting patients who suffer from hemophilia, which is a syndrome that prevents your blood from clotting. A patient who suffers from hemophilia but not treated can accidentally bleed to death as a result of a trivial cut in his or her arm. When treated properly, hemophilia patients enjoy a life expectancy that's similar to that of a regular person. In other words, these clients have all the incentives to keep buying more of the drug that works for them. At the same time, the last thing they probably want to be doing is to go out and experiment with other new drugs. That is what I call "sticky" clients. It's a great niche to look for.

But sticky clients can be found in some other, more cheerful, businesses. A guy who likes to drink a cold Budweiser every evening is not likely to easily switch to a different beer. A person who loves to eat his Oreos cookies with his morning coffee, will not be inclined to swap them for a different product. In general, consumer staples often enjoy that "sticky"-client phenomena, though to a lesser extent than life-saving drugs.

Method #4: "high operating margins"

The next stage in spotting the leading companies in their industries is by diving into some basic financials. The operating margin, denominated in terms of percent, represents the ratio between the operating income of the business and its sales. The higher the ratio, the better, because it means that a greater portion of sales is translated into operating income and not wasted away.

Almost all leaders have something in common. Their operating margins are usually very high, as high as 30 percent and upwards. At first glance, it seems unlikely for a business to earn such high returns. Regulation, fierce competition, and the overall business climate are "supposed" to eliminate such high margins, right? Theoretically, such margins cannot even exist in a capitalistic business oriented world.

Well, the theory is dead wrong when it comes to equity markets and the actual business world. It seems that world-class companies which dominate their industries are, indeed, able to leverage their size to create outsized returns for their shareholders.

Extremely high operating margins are a fantastic indication that something "magical" is going on in the business. That "magic" is attributed to a unique positioning in the industry, or to a well-established brand power which enables control over pricing, or both.

Method #5: Investment in research & development (R&D)

Intel is the global leader in semiconductor (aka "chip") manufacturing. The company researches, designs and manufactures chips for various industries. You can find Intel's "Intel Inside" processors in almost every desktop and data center that uses servers. Although Intel had missed out big time on the mobile revolution, it's is still the most important player in its industry thanks to its impressive innovation abilities. As I write this, Intel had assembled a manufacturing line for 10-nanometer chip, the smallest and fastest chip manufacturing plant in the industry.

It's important to note that, contrary to common beliefs, the semiconductor industry is highly fragmented with many rivals who prefer to design the chips while outsourcing the manufacturing to cheap manufacturers in the east. So, what sets Intel apart from the rest of the competition?

HOW TO SELECT WINNING STOCKS AND AVOID LOSERS

The answer is its investment in research and development. Intel invests a ton of money in its ability to be ahead of the game. Intel's numbers tell the story. The company's R&D expense amounts to a staggering 13$ billion, which equates to about 21 percent of its top line. That's a truly staggering amount of investment that is bound to keep rivals at bay from Intel's pie.

In this chapter, you learned the importance of spotting the leader, or leaders, of a given industry. More importantly, leaders leave trails. You were given five methods that will help you spot the leaders, and the leaders to be. The first method is to follow the market share of the company in a given industry. The second method is to follow the global, highly recognizable brands of the industry. The third method is to spot the companies that sell products to "sticky" clients, those who don't have a lot of choices, or sometimes – those who simply prefer not to choose. The fourth method is to look at the operating margins of the business, and the fifth method is to check the size and quantity of the R&D investment of the business, and its percentage of the overall sales. A business that invests immensely in its R&D is likely building a massive fortress around itself, something that will make it extremely hard for current rivals to compete and overtake it as the industry leader in the future.

CHAPTER 3:
STEP #2: FREE CASH FLOW

My second criteria in choosing winning stocks and avoiding losers is the cash generation capabilities of the business. Cash is king, my friend. And that's why it is so important to watch it closely. And do you know what's better than cash? The answer is cash generation. Whereas the former refers to the cash pile on the company's balance sheet, the latter refers to the capability of the business to generate cash flow from its ongoing operations.

I'll use an example to drive this point home. As of April 2017, Alibaba has been sitting on a pile of cash, 26.5$ billions of it. This was the total cash on the balance sheet of Alibaba, equating roughly to 20 percent of the value of its share. Now, that's very important to know, and it's very comforting to know that Alibaba has an enormous cash cushion for bad times. But the cash on Alibaba's balance sheet doesn't tell me anything about Alibaba's annual cash stream.

If you want to get a grip on a company's cash flow generation, the place to look isn't the balance sheet, but the cash flow statement. When you look it up, you can easily find that Alibaba has generated cash from operations in the amount of 12$ billion, as of May 2017. That's definitely a very impressive amount, but how impressive?

One way to get some perspective on this figure is to include it in a general context by looking at the cash flow generation of the business a few years back. For example, Alibaba generated cash from operations of only 6.6$ billion back in May 2015. In other words, Alibaba almost doubled its cash from operations in a span of two years. That's nothing short of amazing.

Another way to get your head around the cash flow figure is to calculate it as a percentage of sales. All you have to do is to take the sales, or revenue, figure, and then check what percentage of it is translated into cash from operations. In our previous example, Alibaba generated revenues of 23.5$ billion for the year ending May 2017 and 12$ billion of cash flow from operations during the same period. Putting the two numbers together, you come to the conclusion that about 50 percent of Alibaba's revenue is translated into cash from operations. That's very impressive as well since most companies on the S&P 500 translate 10 percent of their revenue, on average, into cash from operations.

Why is it so important to invest in cash gushing machines?

I cannot underestimate the importance of investing in businesses that generate positive cash flows consistently over the years. One big advantage of a business with a strong cash flow is that with cash flow, in contrast to earnings, you know exactly what you're buying into. Cash earnings will sometimes tell you a story that the standard net income will not be able to tell you. Let me explain this point in detail.

Most investors, and unfortunately analysts as well, look at the company's bottom line when judging the quality of the business. Net income is what's left of the company's revenues after deducting all expenses such as the cost of materials, salaries for employees and payments to the tax man. The net income is so commonly used that the most common valuation metric, the price to earnings ratio (P/E), is based on it. It is the net income line that appears in the denominator (the "E).

Net income is definitely something to take into account when analyzing a company. But net income certainly has its shortfalls. One major shortfall derives from its accounting nature. Net income is easily influenced by various one-offs made by the company. These one-time items and other various accounting adjustments often obscure the true earnings power of the corporation. In contrast to net income, cash flow is difficult to manipulate and is therefore much more reliable than income. Trace the cash flow of the corporation and you'll find how profitable it really is.

A second positive for cash gushing companies is their ability to survive challenging times. Business environment, by definition, is very competitive and therefore highly dynamic and challenging. It is cash flow, not revenue that will ultimately help the business pass through challenging times. Take the 2008 financial crisis for example. Companies who entered the crisis with cash flow issues had a hard time surviving it and their shares suffered tremendously.

Take the airline industry for example. Airlines entered the 2008 financial crisis mightily unprepared. A lethal combination of high fuel prices which were a burden on expenses, mountains of debt on the balance sheets and a fierce competition which drove airfares lower – all had a strong negative impact on the cash position of the companies in the industry. There was no way out for airlines. In the ensuing years after the financial crisis, many airlines were forced to file for bankruptcy or merge with other airline companies.

In contrast, companies who enjoyed a stable and

steady flow of cash emerged from the financial crisis barely untouched. Take McDonald's for example. The largest fast-food chain in the world is a massive cash gusher. With total sales of 22.7$ billion back in the year 2009, the company was able to generate cash from operations of 5.7$ billion. That is very impressive, and that's why shares of Mickey D rebounded so quickly after the financial crisis whereas shares of other companies continued to sell on the cheap for years.

A third advantage for cash gushing companies is their ability to exploit opportunities due to their financial flexibility. When assets are sold in the market at depressed prices, cash gushers can come around and purchase them at great prices. Take the pharma sector at the end of 2016 as an example. A combination of reasons such as numerous failures in experiments and regulatory hurdles in the US has caused the shares of most pharma companies to trade at 52-week lows. Now, who do you think can come around and take advantage of such a situation, a small biotech startup or a mighty pharma company that generates massive cash flow like Pfizer or Allergan?

You guessed it right, it's the big pharma who can exploit opportunities thanks to their cash flow capabilities. The same companies can also take advantage of favorable conditions in the debt market and borrow or repay their debt at opportune times for the business.

So now you know that cash flow generation is the metric that you want to consider before investing in a business. Cash flow generation ensures survival in difficult times, provides the financial flexibility to make good deals at opportune times and serves as a general indication as to the true earnings power of the business. But how do we identify these high-quality cash-generating companies?

How to identify a cash gushing business

The most straightforward way to check the cash-flow capabilities of a business is to dig up its cash flow statement and compare it to the profit and loss (P/L) statement. In the cash flow statement, you mark the line that says "cash flow from operations". This number reflects the total cash generated by the ongoing operations of the business over a period of time. Take that number and compare it to the sales (income) that appear at the top line of the income statement.

By comparing the operating cash flow to sales, you'll find the conversion rate. In other words, what percentage of sales is then translated into cash earnings? Any double-digit number is fine, while a conversion rate that exceeds 25 percent is exceptionally good.

If you wish to set higher standards for yourself, don't

stop at cash-flow from operations. If you dig a bit deeper, you will find the free-cash-flow (FCF) number. Free cash flow represents the net cash flow that the company has generated over a period of time, and is calculated by deducting capital expenditures from cash flow from operations (the number we found before).

Plainly speaking, a business generates cash flow from its ongoing operations and invests part of it in building facilities, maintaining stores and other capital-intensive operations. The free cash flow (FCF) figure represents the net cash earnings after all the capital expenditures have been made. In other words, FCF is the purest form of true profit.

I will use an example taken from Delta Airlines (DAL) to drive this point home. This profitable airline generated income of roughly 40$ billion during 2016. If you dig up the company's financial statements, you'll see that it generated cash flow from operations in the amount of 7.5$ billion, an impressive 18 percent conversion rate (I divided the operating cash by the annual income). If you dig a little further, you'll see that the airline invested roughly 3.5$ billion in capital expenditures such as the company's terminal hubs, purchase of a new fleet of planes and maintenance of old planes that needed some fixing. All in all, Delta generated 4$ billion of free cash flow

(FCF) at a conversion rate of 10 percent during 2016. That is a high cash generative company.

In conclusion, cash is king. But it isn't the cash that's sitting on the balance sheet that really matters. It's the cash flow generation that's the ace in the sleeve. Always look for cash generative businesses. They are the real winners of their respective industries.

CHAPTER 4:
STEP #3: SHAREHOLDERS IN THE CENTER

Investing in a dominant leader that generates a massive amount of cash flow is a wonderful start for a stock picker. The next stage is to make sure that the business works for you, the shareholder, and not just for management and employees.

You see, there are plenty of profitable businesses out there. But many public companies often forget who they work for. Instead of trying to maximize shareholder value, they are fixated on striking mega deals to make their companies larger, albeit not necessarily more profitable. Others pursue too generous compensation packages for management and employees, a tactic that often dilutes existing shareholders in the future.

Other companies will not directly and openly pursue the wrongdoings mentioned above, yet they will be reluctant to maximize shareholder value at all times. A classic example of this is the often-heard excuse by management why not to initiate a dividend for shareholders. More often than not, management prefers to accumulate a huge cash pile and not to distribute any of it back to its rightful owners, the shareholders. To put it differently, management sometimes wrongfully aspires to make the corporation larger and more influential. But "larger" does not necessarily translates into "more profitable".

Now, it is one thing for a young company to pass on the dividend and invest it in capital expenditures at the present that will bear fruit sometime in the future. That is totally understandable. But many times, we witness mature companies with a ton of cash on their balance sheet and no idea how and where to invest it.

It is then that management has to take an honest look at itself and decide on the optimal deployment of cash. In many cases, a consistent long-term dividend payment policy strengthens the trust of shareholders in the company and also prevents management from overspending on silly endeavors. Shareholder friendliness is the key here.

Take Cisco, the global manufacturer of data equipment, for example. Up to 2011, Cisco behaved as if it were a minor-league startup despite recording a massive 30$ billion in sales. Management refused to pay a dividend although it was clear that the massive cash generated by the company couldn't be deployed wisely back into the business. Shareholders got the message, realized that management is about to go on a spending spree at their expense and fled the stock. Shares of Cisco underperformed the market over those years.

And then management decided to mend its ways. A hefty dividend policy was launched, and management has increased the dividend by more than 10 percent per annum since the dividend initiation. Shares later caught up with the major indices and then moved to greatly outperform them from the year 2014 to 2017.

Why is it important to invest in "shareholder friendly" companies?

Some companies enjoy a remarkable earnings power due to strength of the brand, operational capabilities, and remarkable execution. But if the shareholder-friendly ingredient is missing, well, then all those wonderful business traits will not necessarily translate to financial success.

It's because of the financial discipline of shareholder-friendly companies. These companies will always do what's right for shareholders, and not for all types of third parties. By investing in shareholder-friendly companies, you align your interests with those of the company itself. Shareholder-friendly companies will not dilute their shareholders with too-generous compensation packages for management, or with dilutive option warrants for employees. This is real money going down the drain.

Shareholder-friendly companies will usually run away from all sorts of mega deals that do not necessarily add value to the companies involved. Instead, they will only engage in well thought out, ROI based, accretive deals that truly add value.

How to identify a company with shareholders in the center?

The main principle that determines whether shareholders are in the center or not is the capital allocation capabilities of management. There are many ways to distinguish shareholder friendly companies. Here I will discuss three different ways of spotting these gems – deal-making, dividend payout policy and share buyback programs.

The first method is accretive deal making. Mergers and acquisitions are the blood of growth. A company can and should grow organically at first. But as the company grows more mature, organic growth stalls, and that's where mergers and acquisitions begin to kick in. A profitable, well thought deal conducted at a good price can go a long way for a company.

Based on my experience, there are two types of deal makers. One type is a company that is always eager to make deals, regardless of price and market conditions. Management wants to control a larger corporation, a mighty influential corporation. Perhaps, a busy mergers and acquisitions schedule might even grant those CEOs with a page on Business Magazine or Barron's.

You should shun those companies, and stay away from investing in their shares. These mega deals are hardly accretive to the bottom line, are usually very expensive, and eventually – destroy shareholder value over the years. A few examples of terrible deals, conducted at a bad timing and dearly paid for, are the acquisition of AOL by Time Warner.

In the example of AOL and Time Warner, the merger was perceived as a revolutionary partnership between two media giants – a content owner and a new- world internet owner. In 2001, the two companies merged in a deal worth a staggering 111$ billion. A few months after the announcement of the merger, Time Warner issued a profit warning and its shares plunged by 14 percent. This was the very beginning of the downhill to come. Eight years later, in December 2009, after almost nine years of nightmares, the two companies parted ways. In less than a decade, this miserable merger destroyed almost 200$ billion of shareholder value.

Another, more recent, value destruction could have

been found in the technology sector. In 2011, Google announced that it was buying Motorola for 12.5$ billion. What exactly did it receive in return for that staggering lump of money? Well, the answer isn't exactly clear. They obviously purchased a few lucrative mobile models, proven almost obsolete a few years later, and a library of patents. As time passed, Google realized that it actually only bought a basket of patents and intellectual property since Motorola's phones were useless and did not assist Google in its fight against Samsung and HTC. Fast forward two years later and Google ended up selling Motorola to Lenovo for 2.3$ billion, a measly fraction of what Google originally paid for it back in 2011.

The second method that you can use to recognize shareholder friendly companies is to take a hard look and see how management treats excess cash. When stock prices are high and acquisitions are becoming pricey, it is a good time to consider the option to return capital to the rightful owners, the shareholders. A dividend policy can do wonders for the capital allocation capabilities of a business, for two main reasons.

First, it prevents management from going on a silly shopping spree. When management is aware that it must pay a quarterly dividend to shareholders, its capital allocation decisions become pickier. Cutting the dividend is a horrible signal for shareholders, so cutting a dividend is almost never a viable option. The conclusion – management of dividend-paying companies must trim costs and focus on maintaining, and preferably increasing the cash flow stream.

The second reason why a dividend policy is good for shareholders lies in the signal it sends to the market. Dividend-paying companies are perceived as companies which enjoy a stable stream of cash flow. This cash flow is later used for dividend payments. It's no wonder that dividend stocks vastly outperform the general market. It's important to understand that they outperform not necessarily due the actual dividend payments. They outperform because the mere ability to distribute dividends on a quarterly basis is a great indication of the company's financial strength. And yes, companies that are financially sound tend to outperform the general market.

But dividends come in many shapes and forms. A third method for recognizing a shareholder friendly company is by looking at the amount and timing of the share buybacks that the company executes. When management perceives that its shares are trading on the cheap, it can go out and buy shares in the open market.

By purchasing its own shares, the company effectively reduces its share count and increases the profit per share.

But one important caveat is in place. If shares are bought at hefty prices, then shareholders will face value destruction in the future. Shareholder-oriented management will use its excess cash flow to purchase its own shares only when shares are a bargain and represent a good deal.

Management of the pharma company Allergan (AGN), provided an excellent recent example for proper execution of a share buyback program. Back in late 2016, Allergan received a payment of about 40$ billion from the sale of its generics division to Teva, an Israeli drug company. Shares of Allergan were changing hands at 200$ back there, reflecting a price to earnings of only 12 times.

That was incredibly cheap considering the fact that the company has been growing earnings at a double-digit rate. Saunders, the CEO of Allergan, stated that he currently sees no better deal in the market than the shares of his own company. Saunders wasn't only talking his book, he actually walked the walk. During the month of November 2016, Saunders launched a mighty share buyback program in the amount of 15$ billion, almost half of the payment that Allergan received from the sale of Actavis to Teva a few months prior to that. Such a decisive buyback, at the right timing and with the right amount of firepower to move the needle, is precisely what is expected of a leading capital allocator CEO.

CHAPTER 5:
STEP #4: VALUATION

How to make sure you're not overpaying for a business.

Picking a great cash gushing business with shareholder friendly management and a good story is a great recipe for success. But if you really want to stack the odds in your favor, you will have to purchase shares at a good price. The actual price you pay for shares will have an incredible impact on the overall performance of your portfolio. As a rule of thumb, I would say that at least 50 percent of the overall return depends not on the nature of the business but on the price you agreed to pay to acquire shares in that business.

I often say to investment advisors that there are two types of mistakes they can make. The first type of mistake is buying into a bad business, whereas the second type of mistake is paying an unfair price for a great business. My word of comfort for them is that the remedy for the second type of mistake is usually time, while the remedy for the first type of mistake is severe loss of capital.

Okay, so I convinced you that a good price is essential to any investment success, but how do I know how to spot an attractive price for a prospective investment?

How to value a business?

Some say that valuing a business is more art than science. I do agree, but only partially. You see, the basis for any business valuation is rooted in numbers of course, but the more experienced you become, the more you learn about certain exceptions and how to avoid all types of valuation traps. So, in this chapter, I intend to share with you the basic types of valuation, and let you take it from there.

The first metric that Wall Street uses when trying to evaluate a business is the price to earnings (P to E, or just P/E). I'm sure you've heard about this metric as it is commonly used in the media as well. Basically, what this metric does is that is takes the price per share and divides it by the EPS (earning per share). Since both numbers are easily accessible, the result (P/E) is only a click away. So, for example, a stock that's trading at 10$ (price) and earning 1$ per year (EPS) will yield a P/E of 10.

What this metric measure is, really, how many years it would take you to "break even" with your investment. Going back to my example above, a share of the business earns 1$ every year and trades for 10$. In other words, it would take me 10 years to "earn back" what I initially paid for. It's a very intuitive valuation metric, and that's why it is also the most commonly used. Calculating the P/E of a business is a good starting point, but the price to earnings also carries its shortfalls.

So, what is regarded as a "cheap" price to earnings and what is regarded as a hefty one? Glad you asked, it depends on many circumstances such as interest rates, economic cycles, and sectors. But I will say anything below a price to earnings of 12 is usually cheap, and anything above a price to earnings of 25 is usually expensive. The range in between them represents a wide array of pricing levels.

A good tool is to always measure a price-to-earnings against the current earnings multiple of the S&P 500, and also against the 5 - year historical price-to-earnings of the business itself. It is always good to know whether you're paying a cheap price relative to previous years, and relative to the overall stock market.

One main disadvantage is that the earnings-per-share could be very tricky. Why? Well, earnings are usually very volatile which is why EPS is highly susceptible to one-off items. In other words, a company can easily record a one-time gain from a sale of a certain asset. This gain might artificially increase the earnings per share and reduce the overall P/E of the business. Therefore, a business that seemed very cheap to us on a P/E basis, might turn up to be pretty expensive – all because of an artificially inflated earnings figure.

Another disadvantage of the P/E metric is the inability to compare valuation metrics across different business sectors. You see, earnings are always affected by interest payments, tax rate regimes, and a various array of accounting terms such as depreciation and amortization. All these metrics make it difficult to compare companies from different industries, or even companies which operate within the same industry but with different balance sheet items like debt and financing.

For example, two companies that enjoy, or suffer, from a different tax rate will end up with very different earnings per share figures, even though their respective pre-tax income is identical. The same applies to companies with different balance sheets. A highly-leveraged company will have a very different EPS figure than a company which doesn't use leverage, simply due to interest payments. In other words, both companies could have an identical operating income but very different EPS figures. That's why EPS is a very good starting point for valuation, but it should always be taken with a grain of salt.

The shortcomings of the price-to-earnings valuation metric, have led to some other useful metrics. One of them is the Enterprise Value divided by Earnings before interest, taxes, amortization, and depreciation. This metric is commonly known as EV to EBITDA or simply EV/EBITDA.

Enterprise value is calculated by adding the market cap of the company (number of shares times the price per share) to its debt load and then subtracting the cash on the balance sheet. Enterprise value represents the real-life cost of acquiring a business. You can't purchase a company by paying the equivalent of its market share. You purchase a company by paying the equivalent of its market share, its obligations (debt) and the cash on the balance sheet.

As to the EBITDA part of the formula – EBITDA represents a rough estimate of earnings, a proxy for operating income. It is far from pure since it doesn't encompass the bottom line like earnings per share do. Nevertheless, EBITDA is indifferent to one- time items, tax rates and financing, which makes it a great metric for comparing companies across different business sectors.

When you compare the valuation of two companies by using EBITDA, you don't have to control for the tax rate they incur, how leveraged they are, or whether they have high depreciation assets on their balance sheets. EBITDA, with all its shortfalls, provides a good proxy for the earnings power of a business. By using EV to

EBITDA you can easily compare European chocolate manufacturer to a US chemical company.

So how expensive is expensive and how cheap is cheap when discussing EV to EBITDA metric? As in everything in finance, the answer is – it depends. For instance, I would never pay more than six time EBITDA for high risk solar companies. At the same time, I would gladly pay more than ten times EBITDA for a business with an excellent franchise and a strong brand. Remember the fantastic call we made on McDonalds back in January 2015? Well, we made that call while the company's shares were changing hands for ten times EBITDA. If you had believed, like many others professionals back then, that ten times is too rich a price for the stock, you would have totally missed the fantastic bull market in the company's shares in the following two years.

So just to give you an approximate ballpark figure for what's right to pay and what is not. Most stocks will usually trade in the range of 5 times EBITDA to 10 times annual EBITDA. If the business is cyclical by nature, like car manufacturers or airlines, don't pay more than 7 times EBITDA. Try not to pay more than 10 times EBITDA for anything unless the business in question enjoys a fantastic moat in the form of a well-known brand or a fabulous franchise. Anything above 14 times earnings is rarely justified and almost always leads to terrible losses eventually. Do your best not to overpay, despite the hype that normally revolves around such stocks.

Most analysts would calculate the price to earnings and the EV to EBITDA of the business, and stop there. It's a pity because the next metric is probably the most useful one of them all. It is a very down to earth metric that is really underused by Wall Street. Perhaps that is why it works so well.

The third metric you should use when evaluating a business is the free cash flow yield (aka FCF). The FCF yield gives center stage not to earnings, which might be manipulated or distorted, but to the one figure that rises above all – free cash flow. The true earnings power of the business. Free cash flow is calculated by subtracting capital expenditures, such as investments in the business, from cash flow from operations. In other words, free cash flow is what's left in the cash register after all bills have been duly paid.

So how do you compute the FCF yield? You divide the FCF figure by the market cap of the company. The market cap can easily be found on any financial website. If you insist on calculating the number yourself, no problem. Just take the outstanding number of shares the business has and multiply that number by the most recent share price. This will give you the market cap.

So, what is too expensive and what is too cheap? I remind you that we are dealing with an FCF yield here, so the lower – the cheaper, and the cheaper the better. So, for example, a business trading at an FCF yield of 5 percent is cheaper than a business trading at an FCF yield of 3 percent. Got it? I knew you would. So, the ballpark in terms of FCF yields is basically anything from zero to 12 or 15 percent. Anything above 10 FCF yield is dreamland cheap, but don't count on finding too many of those. You really need some depressed market conditions to get your hands on anything above a yield of 10. To me, anything above a yield of 5 is very good. Anything below a yield of 2 demands some deep inquiries, so I would normally pass.

The FCF yield is extremely powerful. According to Bernstein Research, one of the leading research institutes in the world, the FCF yield is a great indicator for finding stocks that outperform the general market. Their analysis points that not only is this metric a fantastic indicator for "value at a good price", but the FCF yield is also a signal for future low volatility. In other words, by looking for stocks with a high FCF yield, you are likely to buy stocks on the cheap and outperform the market. And not only that, you will outperform the market with lesser volatility than other, deep value metrics like price to book or price to earnings. Who said you couldn't eat the cake and have it too?

Why is the FCF yield so powerful? That's a great question. I think there are two answers to that question, one is a technical one and the other is more fundamental. The technical answer is that this metric is way under the radar of most analysts and investment houses. You might be surprised but everyone and his sister constantly measures the price to earnings and the EV to EBITDA, because it's so accessible on any financial site, but they go no further. By using a metric not followed by the crowd of professionals, you automatically enjoy an "edge". You can find what's really cheap and likely to outperform.

The second reason is much more fundamental in nature. The cash flow yield doesn't care about sales, about EBITDA or even about earnings. All it cares about is the actual bottom line of the business, or in other words – the cash that it generates. By valuing a business based on its true earnings power, and not based on some tricky accounting gimmicks, you get a real glimpse at the true valuation of the business.

A higher FCF yield is an excellent indication of the cash conversion capabilities of the business. In other words, what part of the revenue is translated into real cash into the company's coffers? The higher the yield, the greater the conversion rate is, and the cheaper the business is. If I could only choose a single metric for valuation of a business, I would definitely choose the FCF yield!

CHAPTER 6
RULE #5: THE CATALYST BEHIND THE STORY

Every fantastic investing idea needs a catalyst to go with it. The catalyst is the theme or the "ingredient" that will make the story work so you can reap the rewards. It is that "extra mile" that will make the stock evolve from being undervalued to trading at fair value.

Never overlook the importance of a good catalyst. You can find a cash gushing company that leads its industry, treats its shareholders well, and trades lower than its fair value. But if you don't make sure that you have a proper catalyst to the story, then the stock you picked might stay undervalued for a very long time. That's not a bad thing necessarily, but most folks do wish to reap the rewards of a successful stock picking analysis. In other words, it is the catalyst that will cause shares to "work" in a timely manner. If you don't neglect the catalyst, and you add it to the other rules I described above, then you are likely to have a winning story.

So, how does a proper catalyst look like? That's a great question. Catalysts come in many forms and shapes. In fact, they keep evolving and changing, just like markets do. The good news, though, is that although history does not repeat itself, the way people behave does. This enables us to draw some profitable conclusions from behavioral mistakes made by investors over and over again.

You might find that surprising, but behavioral mistakes in the stock market do seem to repeat themselves. A combination of herd-like mentality, emotional stress, and risk averseness – all lead to familiar patterns that can be taken advantage of. In this section, I will outline and discuss three main types of catalysts that seem to repeat themselves, in different variations of course, in the market. My experience as an analyst taught me that these three catalysts actually work, which is why I suggest you stick with them. I will first give you some theoretical background on each one of the three types of catalysts, and then I will provide ample demonstration by using real-live examples from my recommendations.

The first catalyst is what I refer to as the "Revenue disappointment" catalyst. The second catalyst is an "event-driven" catalyst", and the third catalyst is what I call a "sector dismissal" catalyst. Each one of these three catalysts behaves differently than the other two, and so is the way to exploit its outcome.

Catalyst #1 - The "Revenue disappointment" Catalyst

The first type of catalyst is the "revenue disappointment" catalyst. Oftentimes, when a company reports a mundane increase in sales, compared to previous expectations, it is followed by a strong sell-off of shares. That's because investors were expecting something more exciting. Wall Street, with its never-ending wisdom, always likes to focus on the top line, aka sales or revenues. In fact, Wall Street usually doesn't care too much about the bottom line, aka net income, as long as sales are growing at a rapid clip.

This perception, of course, is wrong. The bottom line is what matters most in a business, in ANY business, no matter how big or in what industry it operates. Oftentimes, companies cannot grow sales because of pricing pressures, a downturn in demand or any other reason that comes to mind. It happens, and it is a natural course of business dynamics. In fact, the worst thing a company can do is increase its sales by compromising its bottom line. For example, an insurance company can easily increase its revenue by selling insurance on the cheap. The troubles will begin a few years down the road when the lowly underwriting standards will come hunting the company down.

Why does Wall Street repeatedly focus on the top line? One reason is that it's the first number that stands out. Easy-to-extract numbers are often" sticky". These are the numbers that will likely appear on the news and make headlines. After all, who has the time or incentive to discuss the free cash flow of the company when you can easily talk about sales? Wall Street always prefers what's easy and accessible over what really counts but is less available. Therefore, revenue figures will always reign supreme.

A second reason for the street's preference for revenue over net income and cash flow is the obsession that investors have with anything that has to do with growth. A company that grows sales enjoys an expansion of earnings multiple and the enthusiasm of the masses. In contrast, a company that isn't able to grow sales at a satisfactory rate is considered a "slowing" company – even if that miss on sales happened over a single quarter. You can always count on the street to favor growth over value, even though you can really have both if you have just a bit of patience.

A third reason for why Wall Street prefers sales over cash flow and net income is the short-term perception that is so common among Wall Street analysts. Remember, Wall Street lives from quarter to quarter. Looking more than a quarter ahead is considered forever in Wall Street terms. Since sales are often a good proxy for a stock's reaction over the short term, Wall Street accepts that number as the holy grail of investing.

Having said all that, revenue growth is important and I'm not trying to say that it isn't. What I am trying to convey here is the message that very good companies often grow their sales at an unsatisfactory rate. That is, unsatisfactory in Wall Street terms, I mean. The reaction of the street is usually to dump shares first and think later. That is how opportunities present themselves and this is how we capitalize on the first catalyst.

Now is the time for a few real-life examples of how you can profit big time by taking advantage of the first type of catalyst – the "revenue disappointment" catalyst. To demonstrate how profits are made by taking advantage of this catalyst, I will use three real-life examples from Bank of America, McDonald's and Alibaba.

Bank of America – A fabulous turnaround story

Bank of America barely survived the 2008 subprime crisis. When it did survive, with the generous help of the US government, it required an emergency infusion of 5$ billion made by legendary investor Warren Buffett later in 2011. How did it get itself into this situation, and how would the road ahead look like for BAC?

Some background

Bank of America was established 200 years ago, and today it's the largest bank in the world in terms of market cap, and the leading bank in the US in terms of household deposits. After various scandals and bad deals made by management prior to 2010, the CEO was finally replaced with Brian Moynihan who is one of the most esteemed CEOs in corporate America today. Mr. Moynihan was given the task to "clean" the bank from its bad assets, improve its efficiency, and eventually return BAC to profitable growth once again.

And so he did. The most imminent threat lingering over the bank since the subprime crisis was a hanging lawsuit by the Department of Justice against Bank of America, due to the role it played in the financial crisis. The DOJ was seeking some serious damages which amounted to more than 25$ billion. At the end of the day, BAC and the DOJ settled the matter for 16$ billion - the most expensive settlement agreement in the history of the US banking.

The impact

Once BAC settled its lawsuit with the DOJ, the massive grey cloud hanging over its head disappeared. The market did not realize this at first. But looking at BAC in retrospect, this was the turning point for the bank. Legal matters often create a high level of uncertainty around the business, and there's nothing that Wall Street hates more than uncertainty. So, after putting this ugly matter to rest, Mr. Moynihan was able to move forward with his ambitious goals for BAC.

Mending the machine

The first initiative that Mr. Moynihan pursued was tackling the bank's awful efficiency ratio. The efficiency ratio is defined as the ratio between expenses and sales. This ratio tells you what share of revenues, expenses consume. The higher the number, the less efficient the bank is. Back in 2014, BAC recorded the highest (worst) efficiency ratio in the banking system, at over 70 percent.

The mirror image of the efficiency ratio is the bank's rate of profitability as measured by the return on equity (ROE). The return on equity is, basically, how much profit the bank can generate from its given equity base. Due to high costs and subdued profitability, BAC was only generating about 4 percent of its equity, compared to other banks like JPMorgan and Wells Fargo who boasted double digits ROEs.

To tackle the efficiency issue, and increase the ROE, management launched a strategic cost-cutting plan named "New BAC". The plan targeted a massive reduction in workforce and a significant closure of physical branches.

Basically, the bank's goal was to move customers away from the expensive-to-maintain physical branches and into digital banking with high exposure to mobile and internet presence. All in all, the target of the plan was to cut approximately 10 percent of the workforce, close about 400 branches and save about 2$ billion in operating expenses for the bank.

To launch such an ambitious plan, BAC had to rely on its remarkable growth engines. The first growth engine for BAC was its massive deposit portfolio. Equal to 1.3$ trillion dollars, BAC enjoyed the highest deposit base in the U.S banking system. This is of immense importance because being able to hold the nation's largest deposit base enables you to borrow money on the cheap. Then, in turn, you can funnel it into profitable ventures. BAC definitely enjoyed benefits of scale on that front.

The second growth engine was its massive cash flow generation. BAC was minting money and (almost) nobody was noticing the action. Think about this for a moment. Despite the huge settlement with BAC totaling 16$ billion, the bank still finished 2014 with a 4$ billion profit. In other words, despite a very real cash charge of 16$ billion, the bank was still 4$ billion ahead, that's pretty amazing, isn't it?

But the really crazy thing about BAC was how

undervalued its shares were. Because BAC wasn't able to increase revenues over a long period of time, the street totally dismissed its earnings power and the chances that the bank will actually return to revenue growth sometime in the future. Back in 2015, shareholders just couldn't hold the bag anymore. Shares of BAC traded for as low as sixty percent of their book value. That is really cheap since you'd expect an operating bank to trade for not less than its book value.

But it gets even better. Book value includes various accounting terms such as goodwill and other items, which are intangible, and therefore not so easy to quantify. In contrast to book value, tangible book value represents all the tangible assets of the bank, its equity and its business. In other words, this is the value of the bank if it were up for sale on the block, and all its parts were liquidated. Now, back in 2015, BAC was trading at only 80 percent of its tangible book value.

Think about what this means. Back in 2015, shares of BAC traded for 20 percent less than the value of all the parts of BAC. The best description that I can give this is a garage sale being conducted by a drunken garage owner.

The catalysts
Every good story needs a good catalyst. Without a

catalyst, you'll end up with a cheap stock that might stay cheap for a very, very long time. You always need a catalyst for a stock to trade up to its fair value.

At the time of the recommendation, I recognized three possible catalysts for BAC's shares. The first catalyst was an uptick in interest rates. As you are well aware, interest rates have been kept artificially low for almost nine years. That's too long for people to remember that rates could actually go up too. And when they do, BAC stands to profit big time due to its high sensitivity to household deposits.

A second catalyst is the bank's highly profitable trading division. In good times, there's usually a strong uptick in revenue from trading. This, together with revenue from investment banking, can propel earnings to new highs.

Another, third, catalyst is a positive announcement regarding the capital deployment of BAC. As you probably remember, BAC failed the stress test back in 2015 and was therefore forbidden from returning capital back to shareholders in the form of dividends and share repurchases. I believed that any positive announcement on that front may cause investors to rush back into the stock.

BAC is back

We experienced immense success with this

investment. 2016 was a crazy year in the stock market, but it was especially crazy for financial stocks. Due to fears of economic recession from China, the market retreated significantly and BAC shares, specifically, recorded a low of 11$ back in February 2016. But guess what happened over the following year?

Fears of a recession from china receded substantially, and BAC passed the stress test with flying colors and was allowed to increase its shareholder capital return. Then, yields gradually starting to climb up, which led to higher revenue from interest. For instance, a ten-year bond offered 2.2 percent at the end of 2016 compared to a measly 1.6% back in October 2015.

The strategic "New BAC" program turned out to be a success. 18.7 million mobile active users were added and non- interest expense stood at only 13.8$ billion, a decrease of 2.3 percent compared to the previous year.

For the year that ended on December 31st, 2016, BAC reported a net profit of 14.4$ billion (!), the highest annual net profit for the bank over the past decade. In 2016, the bank returned 4.5$ billion back to its shareholders in the form of dividends and share repurchases. And what happened to its shares, you might ask? Shares more than doubled from their 11$ lows and finished the year at 23$. We made more than 100 percent on a conservative bank stock in less than a year. An overly extended revenue disappointment can take you very far.

You didn't expect that, did you? A quick 100 percent gain on shares of BAC

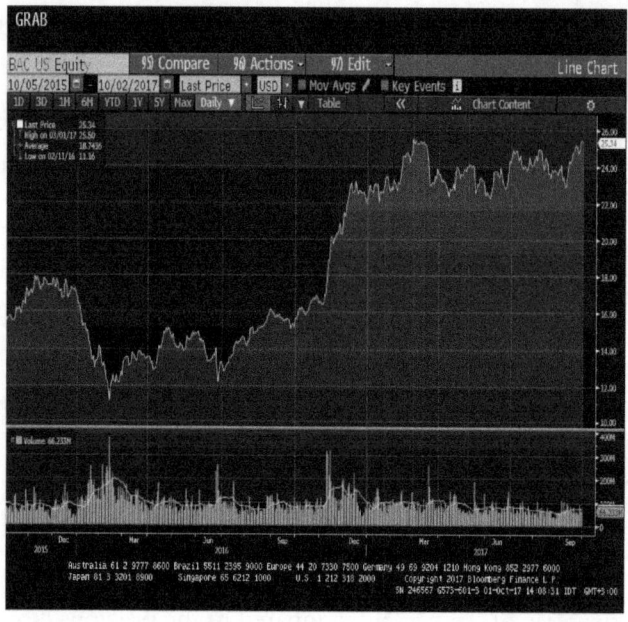

Another "revenue disappointment" story demonstrated by Wall Street is its love- hate story with McDonald's. Fortunately for us, we were there at the right time to capitalize on that wonderful opportunity.

McDonald's –A classic turnaround story

I definitely don't need to introduce McDonald's to

you. The golden arches, often hated, but usually admired, is one of the highest valued brands in the world according to Interbrand, a global consultancy on brands.

Some background

You might be surprised to know that McDonald's has not always been a fabulous growth story and a Wall Street darling. Back in 2013, the company had to deal with a few significant challenges. The first challenge was the increasing awareness of the American consumer to issues such as nutrition and health. Since the Big Mac has never been the ultimate symbol of everything healthy, to say the least, McDonald's had found itself in the midst of a nutrition avalanche. Nobody wanted to eat at McDonald's because it was perceived as extremely bad for your health.

The second challenge was an inner battle within the restaurant industry and specifically, the rise of the casual dining industry. Restaurants such as Chipotle, which serves Mexican food, offered higher quality ingredients and a better dining experience than burger places like McDonald's or Burger King for that matter. Basically, people perceived eating at fast food joints as inferior and were willing to upscale their dining experience for a few extra bucks. It was the rise of what people referred to as – fast casual dining, slowly replacing the fast food dining experience.

The impact

Sales at the burger chain, whose growth was nothing short of outstanding, peaked at 28$ billion and went on sliding from there. As a result of the headwinds I described above, the golden arches recorded 11 consecutive quarters of plunging sales and earnings, with no turnaround in sight. The CEO back then was Mr. Thompson who despite climbing up the corporate ladder from within, was pretty much clueless on how to face these challenges and pull McDonald's out of the muddy waters.

What we saw in McDonald's

Despite the enormous challenges, we saw three very important traits in the company that we had believed would support it in pursuing any potential turnaround in the future. These three traits created a wonderful risk-reward scenario for any investment thesis.

The first trait is its fabulous brand recognition. It is one of the most recognized brands in the world. It's easy to be cynical about Ronald the clown, but his impact on children and adults alike in terms of brand recognition is staggering. It's no wonder that the McDonald's brand is one of the most expensive brands in the world- estimated at a total worth of 82$ billion. You see, a strong brand is a financial fortress for a business. Strong brands differentiate the business from rivals, and companies who own strong brands are able to operate with higher margins.

The second trait is its massive cash flow generation. Despite the gradual decline in sales, the company was generating mountains of cash. Specifically, in 2015, McDonald's generated 6.5$ billion in cash from operations out of sales of 25.4$ billion, an impressive 25% conversion. This ability to generate cash should not be taken lightly and is extremely important in difficult times.

The third trait, and what I believe to be the most important one, is how friendly the company is to its shareholders. A shareholder-friendly company is one that pays a hefty dividend to its shareholders, as long as the money is not immediately required for organic growth of the business. A shareholder friendly company also purchases its stock as long as it is cheap and available on the open market. Moreover, a shareholder-friendly company does not dilute its shareholders.

McDonald's scores high on the shareholder-friendly front. For example, the company paid a total of 3.2$ billion in dividends in the course of 2015 and had invested a total of 5.7$ billion in buying and retiring its own shares in the open market. Furthermore, current management repeatedly stated that it expects to return a total of 20$ billion back to shareholders by the end of 2018. That is an excellent example of a vote of confidence in the business.

The catalyst

And then came Steve Easterbrook. Thompson, McDonald's CEO was forced to resign after three disappointing years at the helm. Steve Easterbrook was quick to come up with a well-planned restructuring plan.

The strategic turnaround plan was based on three initiatives. The first initiative was to simplify the menu. Surprising or not, over the years too many items have been added to the menu. In fact, at some point, you had more than 70 items on the menu. This excessive amount of choice just makes it hard for everyone – for the diner to choose what he wants, for the cashier to take the order and for the cook to prepare the meal quickly. Mr. Easterbrook has put an end to that by trimming the menu substantially.

The second initiative was launching a few innovative products that will "catch fire" among diners. Easterbrook knew that some people like to have breakfast not only in the morning but all day long. They like to eat their Egg Muffin and Omelet at 19:00 PM, not at 7:00 AM. The launch of All-day-breakfast was an immediate success, and that contributed to the top line growth everyone was so eager to see. At the same time, Easterbrook realized that he must put a greater focus on the quality of food. As a result of that, McDonald's has adopted a much higher standard for its meat, and also launched a few steak options on its menu.

The third initiative was going digital. We all live in a highly-digitized era, and restaurants must adapt to that too. McDonald's has launched a series of digital solutions that enhance and expedite the process of ordering and receiving a meal. Today you can use your mobile application to order a Big Mac at a nearby restaurant. Also, while in a restaurant, you don't order from the cashier anymore. You order your meal via a digital board. This makes the order and pick up so easy and intuitive.

The aftermath

Those initiatives actually worked. In the most recent quarter, on July 25th 2017, McDonald's reported outstanding results. The company generated revenues of 6.05$ billion and operating income of 2.3$ billion, an increase of 24 percent compared to the same quarter a year ago. McDonald's reported earnings of 1.7$ per share, an impressive increase of 36 percent compared to the earnings per share of the same quarter a year ago.

The excellent results were supported by an impressive increase in same-store sales – both in the U.S and abroad. Specifically, same-store sales around the world recorded an impressive jump of 6.6 percent compared to the same quarter last year. Even more impressive, same-store sales in the United States, which faces some challenging headwinds, recorded an increase of 3.9 percent compared to the same quarter last year.

The second quarter of 2017 marked the 8th consecutive quarter of revenue growth for McDonald's after three idle years of zero growth. This quarter also recorded the fastest growth in same-store sales in the past five years. Those results were nothing short of fabulous. The drivers behind this immense success were the continuous effort on improving the customer experience at the diners, along with a rigorous cost-cutting plan.

We experienced immense success with this investment. Steve was able to turn the ship around and turn it big time. We initially recommended MCD stock at a price of 90$ a share. As I'm writing these line, shares are trading at 160$ a share, a gain of 85 percent, including dividends, in less than three years on a highly conservative stock.

A Super-size return... 85 percent gain on shares of MCD

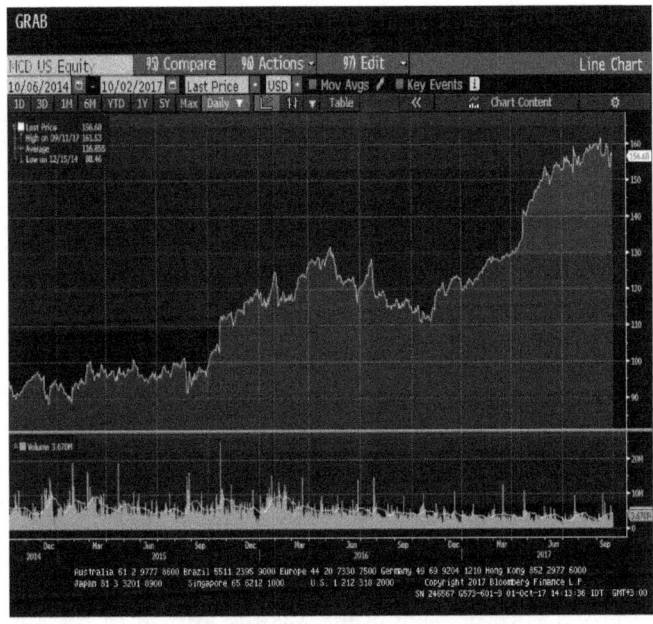

The great Alibaba – go against the crowd

Alibaba was founded by entrepreneur Jack Ma and eighteen other employees back in 1999. Today, it is the leading e-commerce company in the world in terms of total value of merchandise and services being exchanged on its platform. It boasts of a network of over 520 million monthly active users who purchase or sell things in over 200 countries around the world. In the most recent quarter, the total value of all the merchandise and services traded on Alibaba's platform was 570$ billion. So, what's not to like, right?

Some background

Alibaba operates a number of online shopping malls like Taobao, Tao-mall and Ali Express. Some of the malls are for whole-sellers (B2B) and some are for private consumers who purchase items from a store, or alternatively, sell things between themselves similar to eBay. Back in 2015, Alibaba recorded 109$ billion of gross merchandise value (GMV) traded on its various platforms. That is a staggering amount of selling, and it occurred over a single quarter. Just so you grasp the numbers, eBay recorded only a fifth of Alibaba's gross merchandise value over the same quarter.

Especially significant was the growth of e-commerce over mobile which recorded a triple-digit growth of about 125 percent compared to the same quarter last year. In fact, growth on mobile has been so exponential that it currently accounts for more than two-thirds of the total commerce value on Alibaba's platform.

The numbers looked great. Over the period of 2010 to 2014, Alibaba was able to grow sales at more than 50 percent per annum. At some point, Jack Ma decided that it's time to take Alibaba public. September 2014 was the date when Alibaba was to list its shares on the public markets for the first time. The company picked the NASDAQ exchange and received the ticker "BABA".

In the months leading to the IPO, the mainstream media went absolutely insane about the company. The talking heads on CNBC simply couldn't praise Alibaba enough. This overly positive commotion led to an extremely high level of demand for Alibaba's shares at the IPO. If you weren't Goldman Sachs, you simply couldn't get shares. Eventually, shares were priced at 68$ a share, way higher than what the company expected to receive. This represented the largest initial public offering of shares on a U.S stock exchange ever.

Not everything's perfect

Shares closed their IPO auction at 68$. When they first began trading, shares jumped to 93$, nothing short of spectacular. A few months after the debut, shares continued their descent all the way up to a price of 120$. Alibaba was undefeatable. But then troubles began to emerge.

The first trouble had to do with Alibaba missing its quarterly numbers. Instead of reporting an increase of 50 percent in sales, as the street expected, the company performed "terribly" and reported that sales increased by "only" 35 percent. This news definitely depressed investors who sent shares diving by double digits. To the defense of those unfortunate investors, I must add that the company's prospectus, published prior to the launch of the IPO, did show that Alibaba was able to grow sales by 50 percent a year every year for the past decade or so, until it didn't.

The second trouble came in the form of increased scrutiny towards the company's policy regarding forges. For years now, if you wanted to purchase a fake pair of Gucci shoes, Alibaba was the go-to place. It got to a certain point that US Investors were not comfortable with Alibaba's leniency towards merchants who broke the international law by selling forges and violating intellectual rights of branded companies. Soon after that, the US department of commerce issued a warning against Alibaba. This warning led to another double digit decline in the share price.

But the straw that finally broke the camel's back was a strong headwind from China. Back in the beginning of 2016, global investors suffered from severe recessionary fears from china. A bubbly stock market, ground breaking property prices combined with increased level of Chinese regulation – all scared investors away. The S&P 500 lost about 10 percent of its value over two months, but Alibaba, due to its center stage role in the Chinese consumer play, lost roughly 30 percent and traded for as low as 55$. All in all, shares of Alibaba nosedived from their 120$ highs all the way down to the 55$ area. At those prices, this hyper - growth company was trading for only 18 times next year's earnings. And that's when I finally got interested in Alibaba

A lost treasure for a price of a single diamond

The really crazy thing was that all those investors who couldn't participate in the IPO stage could finally get in, for a price cheaper than the original IPO price. Of course, everybody was interested then, when it was practically impossible for the average Joe to buy shares. But now, when everyone and his sister could get in, nobody wanted shares of Alibaba anymore. That's one of the greatest anomalies in the stock market. When everybody wants in, you can't make any money.

Jack Ma reigns in

Mr. Ma wasn't about to sit and watch the share price tank in front of his eyes. He quickly learned the lesson from the rollercoaster at the share price over the months following the debut.

One initiative that he undertook was to tackle the forges on its sites. Alibaba initiated a very stringent policy against merchants who violated the intellectual rights of global brands. Rules were in place and imposed, merchants quickly learned the lesson, and the international community took a deep breath and finally relaxed.

A second initiative that he took was a financial one. He announced a 6$ billion share buy-back program in order to take advantage of the then depressed share price. By doing that, Mr. Ma took a page straight from the playbook of some well-known American CEOs who rigorously purchase shares of their own company when they believe that the price is artificially low. Over time, the reduction in the number of outstanding shares of the company increases the earnings per share and creates value for shareholders.

A third, more technological, initiative that Mr. Ma pursued was the "ecosystem effect". You see, the great thing about companies like Amazon, Facebook or Alibaba is that once they let you into their systems, you're locked. You want to stay in there for as long as you can and do everything you can via the platform. Alibaba has assimilated very advanced big data technologies into its platforms. This big data analysis, via cloud computing, can recognize your needs ahead of time and provide you with timely purchase recommendations and offers. Once you get the payment stage, nothing is more natural than to pay via AliPay, Alibaba's payment system. This is the evolving effect that the ecosystem has on customers, and that's why Alibaba and the others enjoy a wonderful moat and are likely to become bigger and bigger with time.

To Ma's benefit, I must accentuate that all along the way, Alibaba wasn't a pure-play revenue growth engine like Amazon. Sure, Alibaba generated an impressive revenue growth. But even more importantly, Alibaba focused on operating cash flow and a clean bottom line. To drive the point home, all I need to do is to compare Alibaba's numbers to those of Amazon's. In the past year, Alibaba generated 26$ billion in revenues and 11.5$ billion in free cash flow. In other words, 44 percent of its revenue was converted to free cash flow. In contrast to Alibaba, Amazon is a pure top line story, the bottom line is often neglected. In the past year, Amazon generated 150$ billion in revenues and only 9.1$ billion in free cash flow. In other words, only 6 percent of its revenue was converted to free cash flow. That difference between the two companies makes the world.

King Alibaba

For the quarter that ended on March 31st, 2017, Alibaba reported revenues of 5.6$ billion, an increase of 60 percent from the same quarter last year. This marked the highest annual revenues in the history of the company – and more than doubles the rate of increase in sales recorded by the great Amazon.

Even more important than the increase in sales,

Alibaba was able to generate massive amounts of cash flow. The company reported 10$ billion of free cash flow (FCF) in the fiscal year that ended on March 31st, 2017. To further enhance value for shareholders, the company announced a new buyback program, in the total amount of 6$ billion to be executed in 2017.

How did Alibaba do it? Well, the giant sales machine was able to fully integrate its revenue capabilities from various sources, such as mobile, e-commerce and cloud computing. Specifically, the number of monthly active users was 522 million, almost 25 percent higher than the same quarter last year. Today, e-commerce conducted on the mobile platform equaled to 80 percent of total volume of business of Alibaba. To me, it's nothing short of amazing.

And what happened to its shares, you might ask? At the time I'm writing this, shares have literally tripled, from their 55$ lows to 175$ back in September 2017. That was a spectacular growth story that, for some time, presented itself to us at a deep value price.

King Ali-baba... nearly 200 percent gain on shares of BABA

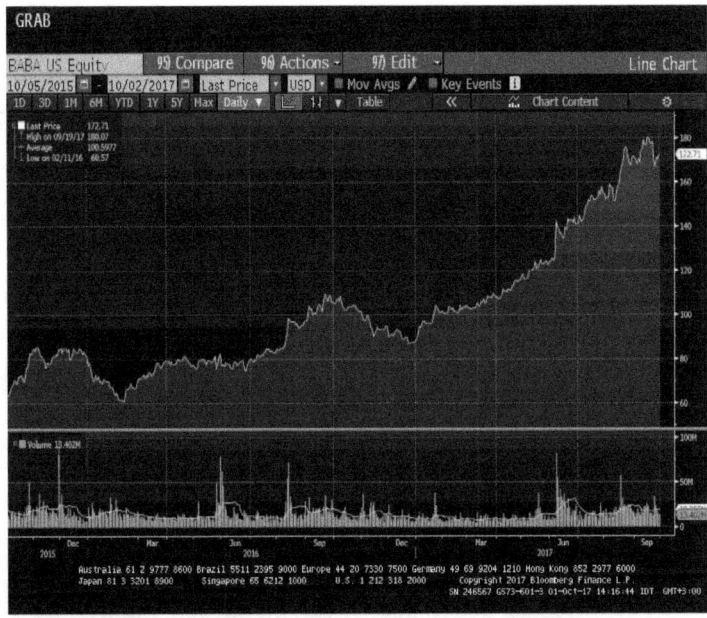

Medtronic – A classic "early disappointment" story

Another venue of opportunity lies in cases where expectations are simply set too high prior to the earnings season. Once the company issues its quarterly or annual report, reality slowly settles in. Oftentimes, it is to the detriment of those who have simply set the bar too high. The consequent share price decline, following the "falling from grace" story, may set us up for a great winner in the ensuing years.

Who are you Medtronic?

Medtronic is a technology company that manufactures and distributes medical equipment in over 160 countries for more than 60 years. Today it is the global leader in the field of medical devices, with a unique expertise in the treatment of cardiac malfunctions. Medtronic performed a transformational acquisition back in late 2014, when it agreed to purchase Covedian, another leading medical device manufacturer that specializes in ER equipment. Following the acquisition, Medtronic is now the leading supplier of equipment to emergency rooms in the US and abroad.

The opportunity

Back in August 2016, Medtronic reported quarterly earnings. The company reported revenues of 7.35$ billion that fell short of analyst's expectations for revenues of 7.5$ billion. On that day, shares plunged by roughly 10 percent and then continued to lose value as analysts were running for the exits and downgrading the company.

Ironically, Medtronic about 15$ billion in market value over the next few months, and that's for a miss of 150$ million in topline revenue. These types of situations only seem to make sense within the realm of the stock market. Obviously, the market overemphasized the slight miss in earnings and underemphasized the prosperous long-term story of the company which was more than intact. It is exactly this type of situation that demands 'pounding on the table' and recommending buying the company's stock.

Shareholder friendliness

On top of the company's impressive cash generation, management was highly devoted to shareholders. Similar to McDonald's, though on a different scale, the company pursued a massive buyback program together with a nice dividend payment. More specifically, during 2016 the company invested around 3.8$ billion in buying back its own shares and an additional 2.2$ billion in dividend payments. That's a staggering amount of 6$ billion that was returned back to the hands of its shareholders in less than a single year, truly outstanding.

Management stated that it intends to carry on a significant efficiency strategy in order to capture synergies between the "old" Medtronic and the "new" Medtronic following the acquisition of Covedian. Management did not just say those words for nothing. It actually proved capable of exploring and taking advantage of those synergies. Specifically, Medtronic harvested 220$ million in synergies during 2016 and stated that it expects additional synergies totaling 800$ million over the next couple of years as it fully digests this mega acquisition of Covedian. We believed this was a great step to make. The share price was depressed and using excess cash in order to perform buybacks is a fantastic way to enhance shareholder view.

The aftermath

A few months following the sharp decline in the share price, Medtronic reported earnings once again. The company reported third-quarter worldwide revenue of $7.283 billion, an increase of 6 percent. Third quarter non-GAAP net income and diluted EPS were $1.553 billion and $1.12, representing increases of 3 percent and 6 percent, respectively. After adjusting for the negative 5 cent impact from foreign currency exchange, non-GAAP diluted EPS increased 10 percent.

So, only a few months later, the company returned to high single digit revenue growth and double digit earnings growth per share. Fears have subsided significantly. The company's CEO, Omar Ishrak stated that "In Q3, we achieved solid results across all of our business groups and geographies," said Omar Ishrak, Medtronic chairman and chief executive officer. "At the same time, we produced meaningful operating profit growth based largely on our synergy programs from the Covidien integration, as well as our focus on operating excellence initiatives."

We made a quick 30 percent gain on a highly conservative company that operates in a highly conservative business segment. It was like stealing a candy from a baby.

A quick 30 percent gain on MDT in less than six months

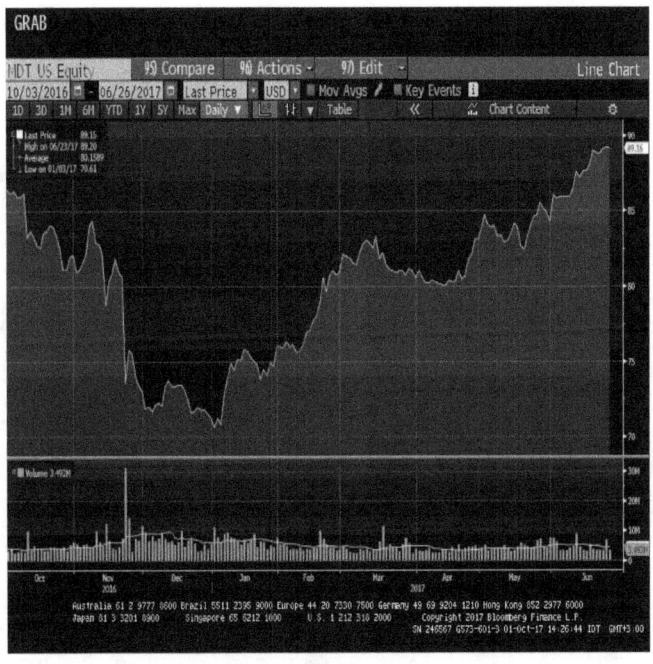

Catalyst #2 - The "Event driven" Catalyst

The second type of catalyst is what I call an "event-driven" catalyst. This catalyst refers to a certain event that is supposed to happen and present a game-changer for the business in hand. There are many different types of corporate actions that can happen in a business. For example, a company can announce a large take-over of a rival in the industry. Another example is a spin-off, a business division being spun off from the parent company and trading as an independent company on the stock exchange.

Although there are many types of event-driven catalysts, there are a few common threads between them. One common thread is that the specific event is very well defined – both in action and in the time frame. An event-driven catalyst isn't something speculative or theoretical. It is something very real which is about to occur in the short-term, but will have long-lasting implications on the business.

Why do "event driven" catalysts seem to work?

There are two main reasons why event-driven catalysts seem to work. The first one is the well-known lack of ability of Wall Street to see anything beyond the next quarter. Complicated business transactions like take-overs or divestitures simply take time. The fruit of the labor will be reaped, but it will not happen over the next quarter or two. Since Wall Street cannot look that far, it usually dismisses the whole thing as "uncertain" and moves on to the next thing. In other words, it takes a lot of imagination and vision to realize what this event is bound to do to the business. This course of events presents an opportunity for us.

A second reason why event-driven catalysts seem to work is that, usually, they are initiated with the goal to increase shareholder value. A company that attempts to take over its rival ultimately wants to become the no. 1 player in the industry and enjoy the economics of scale.

Similarly, a company that wishes to engage in a spin-off one of its divisions ultimately wishes to dedicate greater time and care to its core business. Usually, running a conglomerate with many arms can prove tricky and almost always inefficient. By divesting a business and letting it trade on its own, management will ultimately increase shareholder value. But if we wish to capture the benefits of corporate events, we have to stay tuned to these types of corporate events and capitalize on them.

Bayer AG –A classic "event driven" story

A classic case of a highly favorable risk- reward scenario involving an event driven story could have been found with the world's most famous agrochemical company, Bayer AG back in June 2016.

Some Background

The agrochemical business is simply a fancy word for protection and nutrition of seeds and plants. There are many different sub-sectors in that business, but the underlining thread is that Bayer's products protect seeds and crops from being consumed by pests and fungus.

The agrochemical industry is highly cyclical by nature. Farmers, who are the obvious customers for such products, tend to exhibit highly cyclical purchase patterns. In good years, often associated with rising crop prices, farmers are likely to open their wallets and spend on equipment, gear, and pesticides. In bad years, though, farmers maintain a tight budget and prefer to save the money rather than invest in next year's crop protection. To demonstrate the extent of the agricultural business cycle look no further than the up cycle that began sometime around 2003 and continued all the way to 2010, supported by the raging bull market of commodities. Farmers were convinced that the price of corn, wheat and soy had no place to go but up.

Obviously, farmers were wrong. Sometime around 2010 began a period of consolidation in the market – prices have begun to stabilize and demand decreased.

Then, in the ensuing years, crop prices have decreased rapidly and the agricultural industry has finally entered a bear market. With no end in sight to the plunge in crop prices, farmers were not inclined, to say the least, to spend their money on new innovative pesticides. The whole industry went into a bear market, with the major companies in the industry losing roughly 40% of their market cap in the years 2011 to 2016. When the going gets tough, the tough get going.

Time for some deal making

The crop protection industry is oligopolistic with six companies that control roughly 70 percent of the industry – Syngenta, Bayer, Monsanto, Chemchina, Dow Chemical and Du Pont. In June 2016, Bayer surprised the markets and offered to purchase its American rival, Monsanto for 122$ a share, in cash, which reflects a total deal value of 62$ billion. This is no small change, of course, even for the mighty Bayer.

It turns out that shareholders were not too thrilled with the deal. Bayer's share price plunged by 15 percent on the day the buyout offer was published, completing a 40 percent drop year over year. Monsanto, by the way, was not too impressed with Bayer's offer either. Monsanto's management stated that the price was too low and that they were expecting a much higher bid. In fact, they weren't even willing to "open the books" for Bayer to conduct a due diligence process unless Bayer upped the bid.

Tails I win, heads you lose

At that point in time, we believed that Bayer was an excellent candidate worthy of our investment. We thought there could be one of two scenarios developing. The first scenario is that Bayer does not complete the merger offer, for whatever reason. Maybe Monsanto's management kept playing hard to get. Maybe the regulatory authorities blocked the deal due to antitrust concerns. Regardless of "why", we expected Bayer's shares to bounce back once the merger is called off. That's because the reason for the plunge in the first place was concern expressed by Bayer's shareholders regarding the future of the dividend payouts as well as lack of enthusiasm about the massive debt load Bayer will have to consume to complete the buyout.

The second scenario is that Bayer pursues with the merger. Maybe it ups the price for Monsanto's shareholders to sweeten the deal and maybe it does not. But at the end of the day, Bayer and Monsanto are one and it is important to understand what the combined company will look like.

The Opportunity

We believed there was a great opportunity for success

as a result of the merger of these two giants, and that's for two main reasons. The main reason was that they were a perfect fit – both in the line of business and also geographically. The second reason for this match is an industry-wide consolidation mode.

Regarding the main reason, Bayer was an old-timer in the field of agro-chemistry. Its solutions were effective but they were not groundbreaking. Monsanto, on the other hand, was hi-tech of this low-tech industry. It kept launching new innovative products in the field of genetically modified solutions as well as in other areas. Bayer needed Monsanto to revitalize its portfolio of agro-solutions to best serve its clients worldwide.

The merger also made sense from a geographic perspective. Bayer catered to the farmers of Europe and South America while Monsanto was the go-to-place for North American farmers. A combination between these two giants will enable them to better leverage their existing infrastructure, marketing and distribution to better serve their clients.

The second reason for the buyout is not less important than the first one. The agrochemical industry has been undergoing a massive wave of consolidation over the past two years. In fact, the value of deals in the industry announced between 2015 and 2017 totaled 220$

billion. This kind of wave of deals has not been witnessed over the past 20 years in this, somewhat sleepy, industry.

So, why was it a good idea for Bayer to takeover Monsanto? The answer is simple – economies of scale. The combined entity will be the largest and most diversified agrochemical player in the industry with sales exceeding 60 billion euros a year and EBITDA of over 16 billion euros.

But Bayer- Monsanto isn't only a revenue story, it's also a cash flow story. Bayer's management had announced plans to utilize synergies totaling 2 billion euros. This massive cost-cutting plan will have a positive impact on the bottom line and is expected to generate as much as 6 billion euros of free cash flow a year. This massive cash flow will help the company pay down the debt that it undertook to finance the purchase.

In an industry that is undergoing a massive wave of consolidation, such as the Ag industry in 2016, being the largest player is essential. The largest player is the one able to invest the most in research and development of new innovative products. The largest player can cut operating costs and improve its cash flow capabilities. In short, the largest player will become the one stop shop for farmers all around the world.

The aftermath

Bayer and Monsanto eventually came to terms with one another. Monsanto finally agreed to be purchased for 128$ a share, reflecting a total deal value of 66$ billion. Getting the deal approved isn't an easy task, since the combined entity must file merger requests before 17 different regulators around the world. Once regulators around the world give their thumbs up to the deal, it will be cleared and shares of Monsanto will be delisted from trade. If you're reading this book, Monsanto is most probably already a part of Bayer's agriculture division.

Two things have changed since the initial recommendation of Bayer. One, the market has slowly adjusted to what I call a "new AG world". More global deals have been announced and approved, and the market gradually came to a realization that a market with 8 fierce rivals is about to turn into an industry with only four competitors. Fewer rivals mean less competition. More specifically, regulators around the world have approved the buyout of the Swiss seed company, Syngenta, by Chemchina, and the mega merger between Dow Chemical and Du Pont. These two clearances provided some reassurance to worrisome investors.

The second thing that has changed was the economic environment for farmers. Whereas 2014 represented the worst year in terms of revenue per farmer, things were starting to change on that front. Revenue per farmer has slowly begun to creep up, which represents a healthy proxy for rising sales in the AG sector.

All in all, I recommended Bayer when shares were trading at 88 euros, down almost 40 percent over the past 12 months on the merger news, which was perceived as bad news by shareholders. At the time of writing these lines, Bayer is trading north of 118 euros. We made 35 percent in less than a year on one the largest mega-cap stocks trading on the Euro-Stoxx 50 index.

The lesson

An active market of mergers and acquisitions can serve as a wonderful catalyst for a sleepy industry. Elimination of rivals, via mergers and acquisitions could quickly unlock the hidden potential of companies and increase the ultimate value for shareholders. Outsized returns will usually follow.

The fall and the imminent rise of Bayer... 35 percent in less than a year

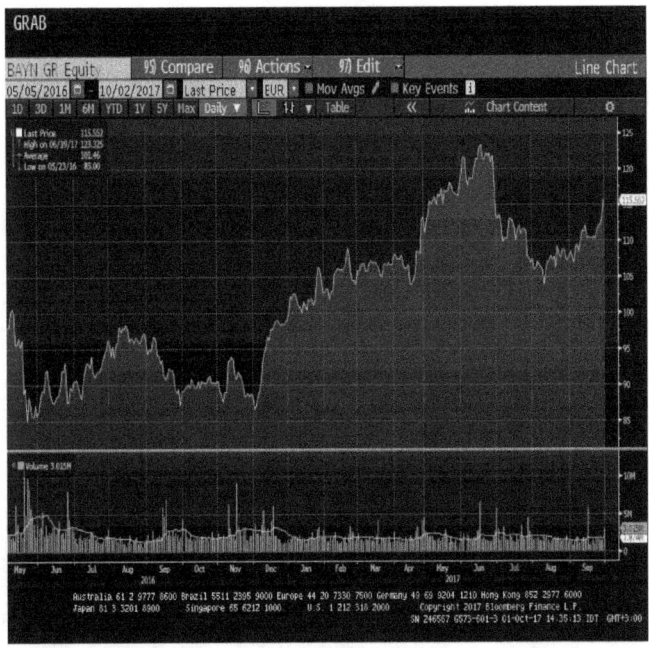

Baxter (BAX) –A classic "event driven" story

Another fantastic event- driven story could be found with the world's leader of renal products. Baxter is a US-based conglomerate that manufactures and markets drugs and medical equipment in over forty countries around the world since 1931. The company is a global leader in treatments for a blood disease called hemophilia, and also in manufactures dialysis machines that treat patients who suffer from kidney failures.

Some background

Back in 2015, Baxter operated under two business divisions – the first was medical equipment and the other was a pharmaceutical division that manufactures and markets drugs and medicines to support patients who suffer from hemophilia. In case you haven't heard of this disease until now, hemophilia is a blood disease that affects the clouting of the blood. Patients who suffer from it might get a relatively shallow cut in their arm and then bleed to death as a result of that, simply because their blood cannot clout fast enough.

This type of patients is referred to as "Sticky" clients because they keep coming back for more. Their treatment is prolonged and ongoing. In fact, patients who suffer from hemophilia enjoy a life expectancy similar to the rest of the population – as long as they maintain their medications. This is why patients that use the medicine often attempt to explore new ways of treatment. If it isn't broken, don't fix it. And that's precisely why Baxter's clients are "sticky" and consistently generate recurring revenues for Baxter.

The transaction that changed Baxter

Baxter has been humming along for decades, growing

sales at an unimpressive rate of roughly 3 percent a year, and growing earnings at a high single-digit rate. Baxter would have gone totally unnoticed by me if it weren't for a very special announcement the company's management made back in 2014.

In March 2014 management announced that Baxter is about to split into two different entities. This split will be finalized by the third quarter of 2015. Following this corporate event, two companies will be formed. One will be called Baxalta and will focus on manufacturing drugs for the treatment of hemophilia, while the other will retain the name of the parent company, Baxter, and will operate as a medical device company manufacturing dialysis machines and personal monitors for patients. Each shareholder of the "old" Baxter share on the record day will be entitled to receive one "new" Baxter share and one share of Baxalta. Right before the record day, before the transaction took place, shares of Baxter traded around 65$ a share.

So how will the new business look like? The new Baxter (medical devices) will generate roughly 10$ billion in revenues with an average revenue growth of about 4 percent and an operating margin of 12 percent. The drug company, Baxalta is a different story. It is expected to generate revenues of about 6$ billion and grow them at around 8 to 9 percent a year. It will also enjoy the margins of a drug company with an operating margin of about 22 percent. Basically, Baxter was the old, mature dividend paying business, while the new drug company, Baxalta will not a pay a dividend but will grow faster and enjoy higher profit margins.

The underlying rationale behind the spin-off is that current Baxter cannot fulfill its potential as one big conglomerate operating both as a drug company and as a medical device manufacturer. You must realize that these are two completely different businesses with very different business dynamics. Current management cannot realistically run Baxter as one solidified unit. Also, in order to grow, each business must pursue its own operating goals and aspirations. Running two ships as one was simply daunting and inefficient, and this has been the main reason for my disinterest in the company for all those years.

The opportunity

At the time, I believed that the spinoff could be extremely beneficiary for both companies. More specifically, Baxter would be able to expand by cutting costs, selling higher margin products and improving its operating margins. Baxalta, on the other hand, will expand by investing in high-end innovative drugs, as well as by acquiring other companies and expanding inorganically. In the years to come, I strongly believed that this spin-off would prove to be transformative for the old boring Baxter and that it would create immense value for shareholders in the long run.

In addition, I believed that there would be some interest from third parties to acquire the businesses individually. Acquiring old Baxter was simply too complicated, but with the two entities trading as individual businesses, everything was possible. This represented an excellent short-term opportunity on top of the long-term opportunity in the transformation of the businesses.

Interestingly enough, the more management discussed the life-changing corporate action at Baxter, the more investors yawned and turned their heads so they could go on searching for the next tech- stock. In fact, investors were so not interested in the story, that they let Baxter trade for only 15 times next year earnings. Another fear that some Baxter shareholders had was the fear that the dividend policy of Baxter will change for the worst and that the dividend payouts will be trimmed.

The aftermath

Not even a single month passed since the floating of Baxalta as a separate entity, and the company was approached by the Irish drug company Shire that offered to purchase Baxalta for 30.6$ billion. The offer was structured as an all-stock deal at a premium of approximately 20 percent above the market price for Baxalta shares back then. But the management of Baxalta refused to be bought out.

A few quarters had passed since the initial purchase offer by Shire. Baxalta reported excellent results with sales increasing by 15 percent quarter over quarter. In light of the results, management even upped its guidance for the year. And then Shire returned to the table, this time with an improved offer. This time, Shire was willing buy Baxalta for 33$ billion, and the structure of the deal changed from an all-stock deal to a stock and cash deal. Shire agreed to pay 18$ in cash plus 0.148 shares of Shire for each Baxalta shareholder.

Why was Shire so interested in Baxalta? The planned acquisition will boost Dublin-based Shire's position in the market for rare-disease treatments, which is projected to grow by more than 60 percent over the next five years to $176 billion, according to market researcher EvaluatePharma. The combined company would generate more than $20 billion in sales by 2020. Also, it would generate roughly 500$ million from deriving synergies following the acquisition.

And what's in it for Baxalta? Well, while Baxalta is a leader in treating hemophilia, competition from next-generation therapies for the condition remains an area of concern. In that sense, teaming up with the 800-pound gorilla in the room sounds like a good idea. Another incentive was the tax savings. Specifically, Baxalta will benefit from a lower tax rate by being taken over by Shire, which is domiciled in Ireland despite keeping many operations elsewhere. The U.S. drugmaker had projected a tax rate of 23 percent in 2016. A combination would yield an effective tax rate of 16 percent to 17 percent by 2017.

Another obvious reason, was of course, the high premium that Shire was willing to offer. Shares of Baxalta traded at a premium of 38 percent compared to the price following the initial debut on August 2015. This time management agreed to be bought out, and shares ceased to trade on April 2016 at a price of 46$. We gained 50 percent in 10 months. It was fantastic.

Okay, so Baxalta was taken out by Shire, but whatever happened to Baxter, the medical device company, you might ask? Well, Baxter was finally free to focus on its core business – medical devices. Without the burden and distraction that comes with running two ships, Baxter's management was finally free to concentrate on cutting costs and developing innovative medical devices.

And that it did.

In the months following the separation from the parent company, Baxter recorded a consistent growth of roughly 3 percent in sales compared to the same quarter last year. Growth was supported by a launch of a new dialysis machine meant to serve patients in the comfort of their homes.

The real story, though, was not in the top line, aka revenues, but rather in the bottom line, in the earnings. Baxter initiated a strategic cost-cutting plan in order to get rid of all the unnecessary overhead. As a result of the implementation of this plan, Baxter was able to record a hefty double digit growth in earnings. Investors gradually began to figure out the story behind Baxter, and to bid up the price its shares. As of June 2017, shares were exchanging hands at a price of 58$, almost 50 percent higher than the price following the debut of "new Baxter" back in 2015.

The lesson

Never underestimate the potential success of a spin-off. Corporate actions like the one with Baxter, almost always increases the ultimate value for shareholders. Cost cutting and increased focus on the core business lead to outsized returns.

Baxter – did you think a 100 percent gain is possible on this boring med stock?

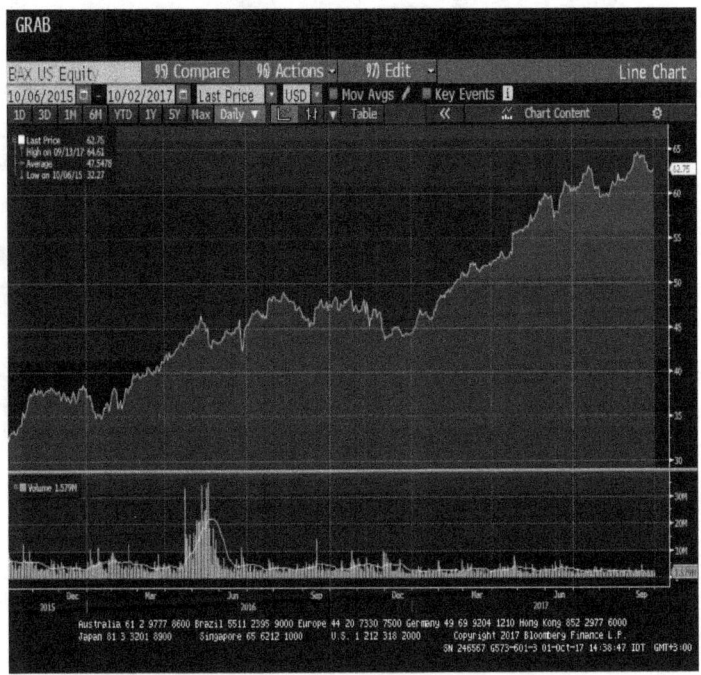

Baxalta – this company hasn't spent a lot of time on the market before being grabbed by Shire...

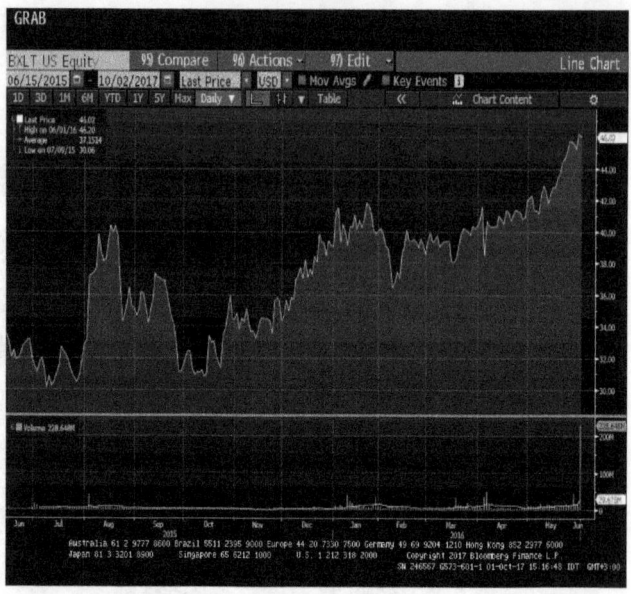

Wirecard (WDI GR) – A fantastic "event driven" story

Not all great stories happen within the U.S territory. Sometimes you have to travel all the way to Europe to get your hands on a great story. But boy, it can really be worth it! Specifically, this story that I'm about to tell you happened in Germany and its main hero is a technology company named Wirecard.

Some background

Wirecard AG is one of the world's leading independent providers of outsourcing and white label solutions for electronic payments. The company develops individual solutions for customers in the retail, service and banking sectors. Wirecard helps ensure secure, transparent efficient and international payment processing. The large array of the company's solutions is designed for offline, online and mobile fields, regardless of the company's scale.

Basically, Wirecard is a one-stop-shop for anything related to payment services. Merchants could easily approach the company and receive a tailor- solution to their specific needs with the highest protection of payment default. More importantly, the technological solution by Wirecard will be integrated seamlessly into your company's sales platform. Can it possibly get any better than that?

Wirecard – by the numbers

Wirecard is a truly outstanding growth story. In fact, the company is probably the best growth stock in Germany and probably in the whole of Europe. Back in 2010, the company generated revenues of 271 million euros and EBITDA of 72 million euros. Fast forward to 2016, and Wirecard is recording more than a billion euros in revenue, with EBITDA of 308 million euros. In other words, the company was able to increase its revenues and EBITDA by more than 300 percent in the course of six years.

These are truly remarkable figures. Even more importantly, the company was able to translate a greater part of its revenues into cash from operations. For example, the company's cash from operations amounted to a negative 23 million euros back in 2010, only to grow exponentially to 355 million euros at the beginning of 2016. The company's ability to translate more sales into incremental cash flow was a great testimony of its mechanism. Wirecard wasn't only about growing sales, it was there to make real earnings, and real earnings are cash earnings.

Of course, shares of Wirecard has reacted positively to the exponential growth the company was experiencing. Shares were changing hands for only 13 euros back in 2010. At the beginning of 2016, the price was already hovering above 50 euros a share.

Because of the company's wonderful management team, consistent delivery of earnings and a clever policy of mergers and acquisitions – you simply couldn't buy shares on the cheap. Normally, shares traded for about 30 times earnings. Not incredibly expensive, considering the fact that Wirecard have increased sales by more than 20 percent in the last decade, but still – shares were not in bargain territory. I kept following the company for years, without being able to recognize a good entry point. Until something very strange happened.

The catalyst – the "money laundering mystery"

On February 24th, 2016 a hedge fund named Zatarra Research, which popped up on the web only shortly before launching attacks on Wirecard, has made repeated accusations via Twitter that caused Wirecard shares to tumble by 25 percent. Zatarra said in the report that it aims to profit from a fall in the stock, which some UK and U.S. hedge funds have also been short-selling.

Zatarra claimed that it has unearthed new evidence that linked Wirecard to money laundering of betting proceeds from offshore poker sites back into the United States, where online gambling is illegal. This was one of the central charges in Zatarra's Feb. 24 report, which runs to 101 pages. Specifically, Zatarra asserted that a British subsidiary of Wirecard, known as Wire Card UK Limited, was the missing link the U.S. Secret Service may have been unaware of during a 2010 probe of shell companies linked to the poker money laundering scheme. Following this report, shares of Wirecard have tumbled sharply, going from the ~50 euro level all the way down to 30 euros a share.

And what did the management team of Wirecard have to say in its defense? The CEO of the company came out with an open statement that "Wirecard is the victim of "baseless" allegations by a previously unknown research firm that has dredged up long-discredited claims of financial fraud". The CEO continued that "We have investigated all allegations. Every single point is wrong. These are baseless," Wirecard Chief Executive Markus Braun told Reuters at the time. "Everything is based on insinuations and false conclusions that are obscured by the complexity of the allegations" Braun said in response to Zatarra's latest allegation. "Old matters are being exhumed that were wrong to begin with."

Our two cents

Such news can definitely get you scared. For a payment processor such as Wirecard to be facing such harsh allegations like money laundry could certainly mean the end of the company as we know it. But something kept telling me that the fund's report is nothing but some hot air that will disappear soon, and that's for the following reasons -

One, we approached numerous investment houses and funds across Europe and nobody, not even a single one could tell us anything about the history of Zatarra. Also, nobody in the fund was willing to accept our call or even provide any means of identification.

Two, the allegations were presumptuous. Wirecard has enjoyed a proven track record of operations dating back a decade. For an accusation like that to suddenly surface, one must have missed the story entirely. Also, we kept thinking how convenient it is to make a claim of money laundering against Wirecard. This type of allegations is extremely hard to prove but its effect on investors is immense. I would say that it's the ultimate accusation.

Three, Wirecard was the right company at the right time. You see, the market for digital payments platforms has just been discovered. We consider this market to be in a supercycle years down the road since this is the field that is partly in charge of the surge in e-commerce. You see, e-commerce could not have surged that far, that fast, without companies providing digital payments. In that sense, digital payment companies are the basis on which e-commerce companies capitalize. Through excellent acquisitions like the Citi merchant and successful joint ventures like the one with IKEA, Baidu, and Apple, Wirecard was able to grab a larger share of the market.

For real or not for real, that was the question. In the meantime, investors voted with their feet and ran for the exits. All in all, shares of Wirecard tumbled approximately 40 percent in less than a month. Finally shares were trading on the cheap for less than 18 times next year's earnings, and that's for a business that increases its revenues and EBITDA at 30 percent per annum. Pretty amazing, isn't it? At that point, we issued a "Buy" recommendation for shares of the company.

The aftermath

Let me make a long story short. Nothing really materialized from Zatarra's accusations. In fact, the only party that was up to her head with litigation was Zatarra itself. Apparently, the German regulator decided to open an investigation against Zatatta and to ascertain whether the fund exploited misinformation to enrich itself by shorting Wirecard's shares.

In the meantime, fast forward a year and a half later. Wirecard AG reported a successful third quarter 2017, remaining on an ongoing strong growth track. According to preliminary figures group revenues in the third quarter 2017 grew in comparison to the previous year period by 52 percent from 267.6 million euros to 406.5 million euros. In the first nine months of 2017, revenues recorded an impressive increase of 42 percent to a staggering 1.022 billion euros

Preliminary earnings before interest, tax, depreciation and amortization (EBITDA) improved by 35 percent to 110.2 million euros in the third quarter of 2017. In the first nine months of 2017 EBITDA rose by 34 percent to 286.7 million euros. Due to the strong organic business development, Wirecard Management Board has increased the EBITDA guidance for the fiscal year 2017 in a bandwidth of between 398 million euros to 415 million euros (previous guidance: EUR 392 million to EUR 406 million).

And what happened to the share price over this year and half since the Zatarra fiasco? Well, from a low of 32 euros back in April 2016, the share price went through the roof and parked at 85 euros a year and a half later. Don't forget that a great "event- driven" catalyst can take you very, very far.

Wirecard −a whopping 150 percent gain in 18 months

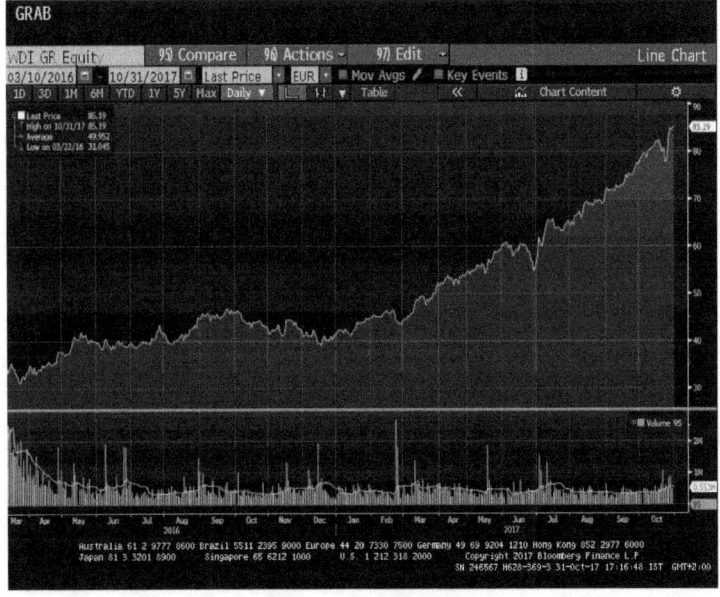

PayPal (PYPL US) – Another wonderful "event driven" story

Unlike Wirecard, PayPal is a well-known U.S based company. Like Wirecard, it serves merchants and individual consumers all across the world and assists them in processing payments. Nowadays, almost everybody is familiar with PayPal's trusted technological platform for secured digital payments, and that's one of the things that make its business model so unique and robust.

Some background

PayPal has a relatively short history as a stand-alone public company. Up until July 2015 it was part of eBay. At some point, it became apparent that PayPal was a true diamond, and that diamond is relatively hidden and only partly recognized because it operated as a division within eBay. As both a leading global technology platform and a financial services business, PayPal required a diverse blend of leadership that could pursue different goals than the goals pursued by eBay. It was time for PayPal to begin trading as a standalone company.

We believed that the thesis for future growth for PayPal as a standalone company was absolutely accurate, and that it's supported by three arguments. The first argument is the immense growth in e-commerce. While brick and mortar stores have been closing left and right, ecommerce has been experiencing meteoric growth of roughly 17 percent per annum, according to Statista, a research firm. You see, ecommerce cannot grow without the technological platforms of digital payments. One is useless without the other, and that's why hyper growth in one of the two sectors will inevitably lead to hyper growth in the other.

The second argument for a successful investment in PayPal lies in the exponential growth of anything that's mobile related. You see, wallets and plastic cards are soon to become obsolete. If you think that I'm joking or exaggerating, please consider the following fact: over 60 percent of the adult population in China doesn't walk around with wallets anymore. They use their mobile phones for everything from texting, buying food at the local supermarket, catching a ride, or purchasing items online. It's so much safer and better this way. Within that context, we believed that PayPal would be a significant beneficiary of the exponential transition to a truly mobile life.

The third argument is the business fortress that PayPal has successfully established over the years. You see, it isn't easy to distinguish yourself as the most trusted brand in the digital wallet space. Issues like safety, smooth transaction and a friendly user interface are critical in grabbing market share from others and turning into the ultimate go-to-place for anything related to digital payments. PayPal has been able to accomplish just that – become the safest and most trusted payment platform in the world.

The way I saw it, PayPal has so many ways to win. It could increase the number of its individual users or it could increase the number of its merchants on its platform, or probably both. Another way to capture outsized market share is by increasing the average size of a transaction, or even expanding its revenue sources by offering credit to its consumers or to its merchants.

PayPal – by the numbers

PayPal is a rapidly growing global leader in digital payments and the most trusted digital wallet, with more than 152 million active registered accounts prior to the separation from the parent company, eBay. Prior to the debut, accounts grew 15% year-over-year last quarter. Revenue over the last 12 months grew by 19% over the prior year period to approximately $7.2 billion.

PayPal facilitates one in every six dollars spent online today. Total payments volume over the last 12 months increased by 26% to $203 billion, providing merchants and consumers worldwide a faster, safer way to pay and be paid. PayPal is fully localized in 26 currencies, is available in 203 markets worldwide and has relationships with 15,000 financial institutions. Representative of its global reach, PayPal is the No. 1 payments processor for business to consumer exports for Chinese merchants.

With acquisitions such as Braintree and its new One Touch mobile payments experience, PayPal continues to lead and innovate in mobile payments. You see, One Touch is the industry's first and only single touch payments experience.

But investors yawned...

Considering the extent of opportunities PayPal was facing, you might think investors would fall over one another to buy shares. Well, that was hardly the case. Shares were first offered at 38$ a share during the debut on July 2015 and the share price drifted around that range ever since. In fact, when markets switched to a "risk off" mode back in February 2016, PayPal's shares traded for as low as 30$ a share. It was amazingly cheap.

In fact, given revenues of 9.2$ billion and earnings per share of 1.25$, Shares of PayPal were trading for 5 times annual revenues and 28 times earnings per share. Now, that's not cheap in absolute terms, but compared to other growth stocks in the sector, PayPal was in fact very cheap. For comparison, Shares of Visa were trading for 13 times sales and 35 times earnings per share, while shares of MasterCard were trading for 11.5 times sales and 28 times earnings per share.

It was somewhat of a strange situation where investors decided they want to stick with the "old and tested" stocks of Visa and MasterCard and not go for well-oiled growth machine of PayPal. Ironically, investors were willing to bid up the prices of the former two although they were mature companies operating in a mature industry of credit cards, while not giving enough credit for the new growth player in the new industry of digital payments.

We strongly believed that Mr. Market hasn't realized that the spin-off from eBay would be a game-changer for both companies. After all that time, PayPal has finally emerged as a pure play on digital payments, and with a stunning record of a consistent double digit growth – both in revenues and in earnings, should be revalued by the market.

PayPal proves to the world that it's a diamond.

PayPal has steadily increased its market share in the digital payment space, with revenues increasing at 30 percent year in year out. For example, in the third quarter of 2017, PayPal generated revenues of 3.23$ billion and earnings of 46 cents per share. These numbers represented an increase of 21 percent and 31 percent, respectively, compared to the third quarter of 2016.

The growth in PayPal's top and bottom line were supported by a substantial increase in the number of its users as well as an increase in the total transaction volume (TV) generated on its platform. In the third quarter of 2017, PayPal processed 1.9 million transactions on its platform, amounting to a total payment volume of 114$ billion. These transactions were processed from 218 million accounts of the company's active users.

Even more important to us, PayPal's growth wasn't just a classic top- line growth. In fact, PayPal's massive growth was also deeply rooted in the bottom. During that third quarter of 2017, PayPal generated 1$ billion of cash flow from operation and 841$ million of free cash flow (FCF). In other words, revenues were quickly translated into earnings and cash flow.

What we perceived as truly outstanding was PayPal's ability to create joint ventures (JV) and partnerships across the world that enhances value. One example of a successful partnership was PayPal's agreement with Skype users who can now send and receive cash payments safely by using PayPal's mobile activity. Another example is PayPal's long term partnership with MasterCard that began in Europe but quickly expanded to Canada and Latin America. And of course, one of the most prominent achievements of PayPal recently was its partnership with Apple who agreed to integrate PayPal's "Pay with PayPal" button in its new iPhones.

PayPal – the aftermath of things

PayPal has been delivering excellent results, consistently beating analyst's estimates quarter after quarter. It has never carried any debt on its balance sheet since its spin- off from eBay, it was generating mountains of cash, and it was growing revenues at more than 25 percent per annum. Finally, it was time for investors and analysts alike to adjust their previous estimates in order to reflect PayPal's outstanding execution. And with that, shares of PayPal finally enjoyed an earnings multiple expansion that they deserved. After the dust settled, we made nearly 100 percent on PayPal's shares in a little over two years.

Watch out eBay, PayPal is behind you – a 100 percent gain in 24 months

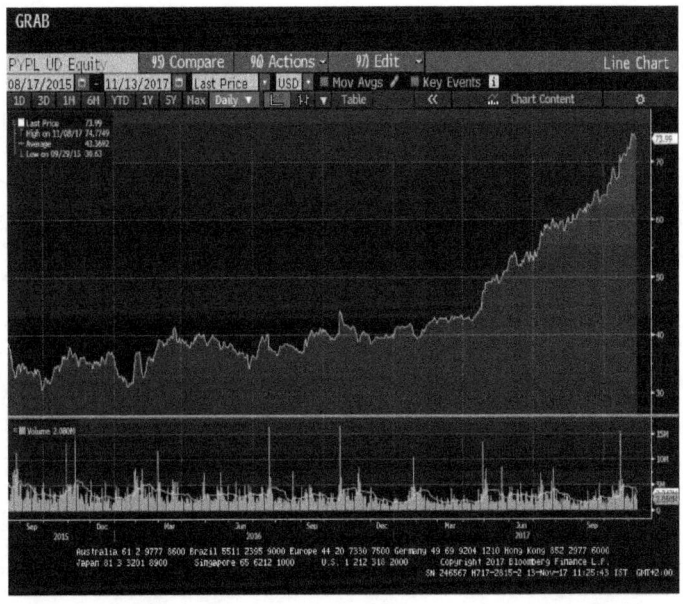

Catalyst #3 - The "Sector driven" Catalyst

So, the first type of catalyst is a "revenue disappointment" catalyst. The second catalyst is an "event-driven" catalyst. Now, we have the third catalyst – the "sector driven" catalyst. This catalyst takes place when a whole sector is under fire. Investors are dumping shares of companies in the sector, regardless of the specific merits that an individual company may have. In other words, investors are overly pessimistic on a sector and they're selling left and right.

There could be numerous reasons why the market decides to dump a whole sector in its entirety. Sometimes the end product becomes obsolete and outdated. At other times, a whole sector might receive some serious regulatory scrutiny. In other cases, especially in the oil and mining sector, prices of oil or gold might tank, which may cause some serious devaluation of the whole sector.

Although there are many different reasons for "sector driven" catalysts, there are a few common threads between them. One common thread is that all the companies in the industry suffer from almost no exceptions -The great ones, along with the mediocre ones. This isn't just a bad earnings-report by one company or another. I'm talking about some mega across-the-board suffering of most, if not all, companies which operate in that sector. Usually, stocks in the sector will lose anywhere between 10 percent and 20 percent before you can safely announce that this is, indeed, a sector-wide event.

A second common thread is the general dislike of investors towards investing in the sector. Usually, the sector-wide decline in share prices enhances further selling, causing a vicious cycle of a downhill slope. By then, the media is obsessed with the sector. You'll probably watch the talking heads on CNBC discuss the "imminent demise" of the sector altogether, and why you shouldn't invest one penny in it. Of course, this is usually the best time to invest in the sector.

Delta Airlines and the airline industry

Delta Airlines was founded in 1928 in the United States and today it is the most profitable airline among US airlines. Thanks to its impressive presence among business customers in NY hubs, and thanks to its quality of service, Delta has won the title- "The most admired Airline Company in the world" for five straight years. Delta flies to 335 different destinations globally, across 60 countries and 6 continents. Today, Delta operates more than 800 airplanes, employs more than 85,000 employees and trades at a market cap in excess of 35$ billion.

The industry – the challenges

Back in 2016, the airline industry has been facing a number of challenges. The first challenge was the price of oil which is one of the most significant expenses for the industry as a whole. The price for an oil barrel, bottoming at around 25$, has spiked towards 40$ a barrel. That is a very significant increase occurring in a very short period of time, and it punctures the bottom line significantly. Some companies, like American Airlines, do not hedge against the oil price. These companies, and their shares, have suffered accordingly.

Another challenge at the time was the fierce competition in the industry. Several airlines have made substantial purchases of new planes, thereby increasing their fleet. This has caused some fears in the industry of a "price war" among airlines, which might drive down ticket prices and lower the revenue per passage, a closely watched profitability metric in the industry.

The opportunity

So yes, the airline industry has been suffering from some terrible headwinds. But the cup is also half full. Let's look at a few bright points in the industry. First, the airline industry is heavily impacted by oil price which is the source of jet fuel, the main cost of the industry. Back in 2014, when oil traded for more than 110 dollars a barrel, operating conditions were challenging for the industry as a whole. Fast forward to 2017, oil is currently trading south of 50$ a barrel. With expenses trimmed substantially, the bottom line improved significantly.

Take Delta Airlines, for example. Back in 2010, Delta generated 4.1$ billions of EBITDA and earnings of 1.7$ per share. Fast forward seven years and Delta is recording EBITDA of 8.4$ billion and earnings of 4.6$ per share. In other words, Delta was able to triple its earnings per share because the oil price has halved during the same period. In other words, the significant decline in the oil price definitely helped airlines improve their bottom line.

Another bright spot in the airline's industry was the change in business mentality. In tough times, complacency has gone out the window and has been replaced by a strict budgetary discipline. Airlines aren't flying planes in the air simply to generate traffic; they're there to make a profit. This might sound obvious to you, but I'm talking about a fundamental change in the business paradigm of the industry. You see, airlines will not sacrifice their bottom line (earnings) for their top line (revenues) anymore.

Another big positive for Delta Airlines was the way the company treated its shareholders. Delta's management has always treated its shareholders with respect. Over the past two years, Delta has paid 600$ million in dividends to its shareholders. More importantly, management hasn't been sitting on its hands waiting for the share price to recover. It took advantage of the depressed share price and was buying back shares, lots of shares. Over the past two years, Delta has invested a total of 3.3$ billion in buying back its own shares. This has helped to lift the earnings per share of Delta by over 10 percent over the same period of time. Lately, the company has announced that it intends to return 70 percent of the annual free cash flow back to its shareholders.

The share price – a wonderful entry point

The fears surrounding the airline industry have caused airline shares to drop significantly, underperforming the S&P 500 by more than 30 percent. That's quite an underperformance. Specifically, shares of Delta Airlines traded for less than six times net earnings, or 3.5 time annual EBITDA (operating earnings). Shares of Delta haven't been that cheap since the colossal Armageddon of airlines back in 2010. For us, Delta represented a wonderful opportunity at the time, and we initiated a "Strong Buy" on its shares back in August 2016 at a price of 35$ a share.

But apparently, we weren't the only ones who were excited by the opportunity that presented itself in the airline industry. Warren Buffett, the CEO and major owner of Berkshire Hathaway, disclosed later in November that year that he bought into several airlines during the months of August and September. Buffett, a known "hater" of the airline industry, claimed that airlines are finally a good investment at current valuations. More importantly, airlines have turned into cash gushing machines, turning a significant part of their revenues into earnings and cash flow. Needless to say, we agreed with every word he said.

The aftermath

A year has passed since our initial recommendation, and the market quickly realized that business conditions in the airline industry have tremendously changed for the better. Airlines have been enjoying the relatively low oil price, turning a greater part of their revenue stream into earnings. Even more importantly, Airlines have generated unprecedented amounts of cash flow, and returning them to their shareholders in the form of dividends and buyback of shares.

Fast forward a year and shares of the airline's carriers have appreciated significantly. Specifically, Shares of Delta Airlines have risen from 35$ back in August 2016, to 55$ in June a year later. We booked a profit of almost 60 percent in less than a year.

Is it a bird? Is it superman? No, it's Delta Airlines with a 60 percent gain...

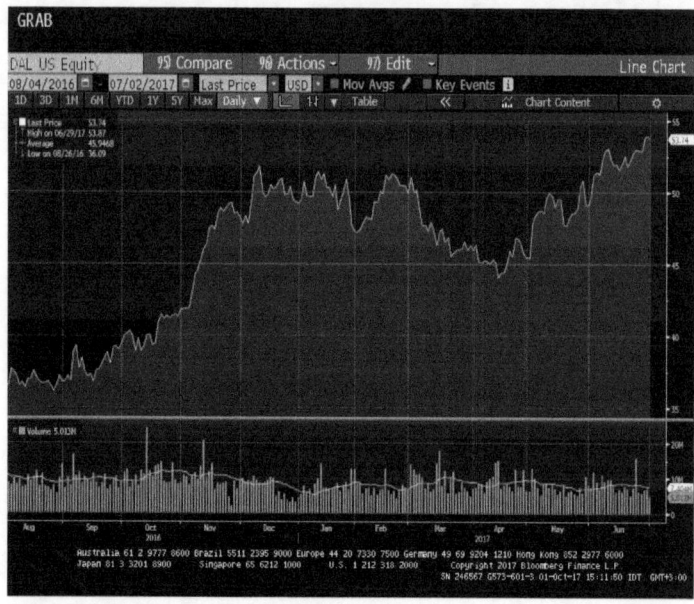

CBS and the media industry

Another classic case of a highly favorable risk- reward scenario evolving a whole industry was the case for media stocks back in 2015. That year was the most successful year of Netflix (NFLX), the leading company in the field of video streaming and online content. Netflix reported record earnings, and most importantly in the industry, a record increase in the number of subscribers. Netflix was king and everybody and his sister worshiped the king. Supported by these fancy figures, Netflix reported a record year in terms of sales and earnings.

The challenge and opportunity

Warmed to the idea of the rise in online video and television streaming, the investing community was quick to rule that the "old" and traditional media is no longer relevant. Shares of media companies such as Fox, Time Warner and CBS have fallen sharply, ending the year down by an average of 40%. The higher everybody regarded Netflix, the more contempt they showed to traditional media players like FOX, CBS, Time Warner and the likes. The conventional theme was that subscription Video on Demand (SVOD) was going to kill advertising revenue from TV and local broadcasting networks, and that the whole industry was doomed. As a result of this, media stocks lost, on average, a staggering 40 percent of their value during 2015. It was an impressive bloodbath and no one was spared.

Who are you, CBS?

CBS Corporation was founded in 1928 as a result of a merger between 16 local radio stations. Today, it is one of the three leading broadcasting networks in the US. It generates revenue from its media division through CBS Films and CBS Network (60 percent of revenue), its television and radio divisions (20 percent of revenue), broadcasting packages such as CBS Sports and Showtime

(14 percent) and publication division through Simon & Schuster (6 percent of revenue).

In the past twelve months ending June 2017, CBS generated revenues of 13.5$ billion and EBITDA of 3.15$ billion. Cash flow from operations amounted to 1.37$ billion, roughly 10 percent of total sales – that was a pretty impressive conversion rate. But investors were wary of media stocks, and CBS was no exception. Valuations in the industry had reached lows not seen in almost a decade. In particular, CBS traded for only 10 times annual earnings while generating about 1.1$ billions of free cash flow (FCF) every year. The stock was hammered and was getting ridiculously cheap.

Shareholder friendliness

On top of the company's impressive cash generation, management was highly devoted to shareholders. Similar to McDonald's, though on a different scale, the company pursued a massive buy-back program together with a healthy dividend payment. More specifically, in the years 2012 to 2015 the company invested 7$ billion in buying back its own shares and an additional 1$ billion in dividend payments to its shareholders.

Management further stated that it intends to invest an additional 5$ billion in share buy- backs over the next three years. We believed this was a great step to make. The share price was depressed and using excess cash in order to perform buy backs was a fantastic way to enhance shareholder value. We picked CBS as our favorite candidate in the "old & Conventional" media space.

Recovery plan

The company's management was highly seasoned in the media business environment and it didn't just sit idle and watch the runaway from traditional media. It has implemented few initiatives over the past three years to better cope with the changing business climate in the media space. The first initiative was to gradually decrease the company's dependency on advertising as a percentage of total sales.

You see, advertising revenue is extremely cyclical and is therefore greatly affected by the business climate and by the tendency of companies to spend few extra dollars on promotion, which is something whose results are not felt immediately. Specifically, revenue from advertising represented more than 70 percent of CBS's revenue a few years back. But now, management is keen to reduce it to a more manageable 50 percent of sales. To compensate for the missing revenue source, management has invested a lot of effort in improving its content. Selling high-quality content is an excellent source of revenue since it isn't as dependent on the economic climate as revenue from advertising. By doing so, CBS is turning the ship and becoming more and more immune to outside noise.

The second initiative was to boost another revenue engine, called retransmission fees. CBS, like other players in the industry, are able to charge hefty fees from the cable companies for the actual transmission of the content, and that's in addition to charging them for the content itself. As an illustration, content companies like CBS are able to charge cable companies 1$ per subscriber per month. This fee is expected to increase over the years and reach 4$ per subscriber per month by 2020. Retransmission fees represent a high margin revenue stream, like making money out of thin air.

The aftermath

You didn't have to be a genius to go long CBS at the end of 2015. There was nothing wrong with the business and there was nothing wrong with management, and yet shares were attractively priced at the time. The only feasible obstacle facing the company then was a terrible investor sentiment towards conventional media in general, versus the tremendous success that Netflix was experiencing.

CBS had the three essentials of a successful investment-high-quality management, shareholder friendliness, and a depressed stock price as a result of negative public sentiment. High quality, cash generative firms are likely to weather the temporary storm. The stock rebounded very quickly thereafter, recording more than 50 percent gain less than a year later.

CBS – a great media play… with a 50 percent gain

CHAPTER 7:
SOME FINAL THOUGHTS

The stock market has taught me, over and over again, that there isn't a single holy- grail method that works all the time. And if somebody tries to convince you that such a method does exist, do yourself a favor and stay away from him and his money. This type of science is highly hazardous for your health and wealth.

The ultimate goal of this book is to provide you with what I truly believe to be the best essential toolkit out there. Of course, I could have given you twenty rules, but that's too easy. Writing about the ultimate five investing rules is much harder.

If the stock market were a road, then these five investing rules are the best way to make it home safely. By following the first investing rule, the "dominant position" rule – you make sure that the car you're driving is mechanically sound and capable of driving you from point A to point B. Companies that enjoy a dominant position in their field are likened to a mechanically sound automobile.

By following my second rule, the "cash flow" rule, you will never run out of gas. A stream of cash flow to a company is as important as gas to a car. That's what's making it tick. Without gas, you could drive a Ferrari but still get yourself stuck up a hill on some deserted road. Cash flow, and not necessarily earnings, is the lifeblood of companies.

By following my third rule, the "shareholder-friendly" rule, you won't stumble upon a non-trustworthy driver. You see, shareholder friendly management behind the helm is precisely what you need to drive you from point A to point B safely. In that sense, a shareholder-friendly management is a reliable driver working for you.

By following my fourth rule, "the catalyst", you make sure that the car will arrive home safely by complying with traffic signs and using a proper navigation system. You see, shares could stay cheap longer than you can stay solvent. By following the right catalyst, aka using a proper navigation system, you will make sure that the car is, indeed, driving in the right direction.

And finally, by following my fifth rule, "valuation of the business", you make sure that the drive is, in fact, worth it financially. You can drive from anywhere to anywhere but as long as pricing and budget are not strictly maintained, the drive will not be economically sound eventually.

Stick to my five steps – learn them, learn them over again, and then implement them in the real-time world of the markets.

Successful investing to you,

Shmulik Karpf

www.ingramcontent.com/pod-product-compliance
Lightning Source LLC
Chambersburg PA
CBHW050304230526
45471CB00005B/2012

9781987592856